W9-AUG-133

THE FAIRFAX
EXPERIENCE

THE FAIRFAX EXPERIENCE

WHAT THE MANAGEMENT TEXTS DIDN'T TEACH ME

FRED HILMER
WITH BARBARA DRURY

BICENTENNIAL
1807
WILEY
2007
BICENTENNIAL

John Wiley & Sons Australia, Ltd

First published 2007 by
John Wiley & Sons Australia, Ltd
42 McDougall Street, Milton, Qld 4064

Offices also in Sydney and Melbourne

Typeset in Bembo 12/14.8pt

© Fred Hilmer 2007

The moral rights of the authors have been asserted

National Library of Australia Cataloguing-in-Publication data:

Hilmer, Frederick G. (Frederick George), 1945- .

The Fairfax experience: what the management texts didn't teach me.

Includes index.

ISBN 9 7807 3140 5626.

ISBN 0 7314 0562 5.

1. Hilmer, Frederick G. (Frederick George), 1945- . 2. John Fairfax Limited
- Management. 3. Newspaper publishing - Australia - Management. 4.
Organizational change - Management. I. Drury, Barbara. II. Title.

658.406

Back cover photograph © Anthony Browell. Reproduced with permission

Fairfax Syndications reproduced with the permission of Fairfax

'How Some Bosses Fix a Company in Crisis' by Peter Holder and Jo Casamento, *The Daily Telegraph*, 24/1/01 © News Limited

Extract from RG Hagstrom Jr, *The Warren Buffett Way*, on p. 171 reproduced with the permission of John Wiley & Sons, Ltd

Cover design by Alison Fraser

Printed in Australia by McPherson's Printing Group
10 9 8 7 6 5 4 3 2 1

Disclaimer

Contents

About the author   vii

Preface   ix

Introduction: On becoming a rat   1

1 An off-the-wall appointment   11

2 The success Holy Grail   35

3 The Fairfax experience   53

4 In the hot seat: the decision environment   87

5 The positive bias   107

6 Being positive about negatives   133

7 Lessons for leaders and educators   157

Postcript: Media reform   167

Appendix A: Fairfax share prices compared with Rural Press and Seven
    Network share prices   173

Appendix B: International newspaper companies — annualised total
    shareholder returns 1998–2005   174

Appendix C: The Buffett tenets for success   175

Appendix D: The classic textbook formula for success   176

Appendix E: Fairfax's organisational structure — 1998   177

Appendix F: Fairfax's organisational structure — 1999   178

Appendix G: Fairfax's organisational structure — 2003–2004   179

Appendix H: Fairfax's organisational structure — 2005   180

Appendix I: Sample pages from my 2004 business diary   181

Notes   183

Index   185

*To my family who put up with me not only during the
writing of this book but also through the
seven years on which it is based.*

About the author

Fred Hilmer (AO) was the chief executive officer of John Fairfax Holdings Limited from 1998 to 2005. He was appointed the vice chancellor and president of the University of New South Wales in October 2005 and took up that position in June 2006.

Prior to joining Fairfax he was the dean and director of the Australian Graduate School of Management (AGSM) in the University of New South Wales and a director of Port Jackson Partners Limited. Before joining AGSM Fred was a director of McKinsey & Company, at which he was responsible for managing the Australian practice. He holds a degree in law from the University of Sydney, a Master of Laws (LLM) from the University of Pennsylvania and a Master of Business Administration from the Wharton School of Finance, where he was appointed a Joseph Wharton Fellow. In 1991 the Australian Institute of Management awarded him a special John Storey medal for distinguished contribution to the advancement of management thinking in Australia.

Earlier in his career Fred was a member of the Faculty of Law at the University of Pennsylvania and he also practised law in Australia. He served on the Committee of Inquiry into Management Education during 1981 and 1982.

Fred was a member of the Commonwealth Higher Education Council and chair of the Business Council of Australia's Employee Relations Study Group. In 1992 and 1993 he chaired the National Competition Policy Review Committee. He is the lead independent director of Westfield Holdings Limited. He previously served as the chair of Pacific Power, the deputy chair of Foster's Group Limited and as a director of a number of other Australian companies.

He has written extensively on strategy, organisation and economic reform and is the author of a number of books, including *When the Luck Runs Out* and *New Games/New Rules*, and co-author of *Strictly Boardroom*, *Working Relations* and *Management Redeemed*.

Preface

After I had been chief executive officer (CEO) of Fairfax for some six years, I was approached by a producer from ABC television. He was interested in making a program on the real-life job of a CEO. Chief executives, he said, are increasingly public figures. Their activities, consumption patterns, political allegiances and views on policy, not to mention their pay and social lives, are often in the news.

However, the producer felt that this public face of the CEO was only part of the story, and probably the least important part. What is not well understood is what CEOs do all day—how they make decisions, lead their troops, work with stakeholders, obtain information and communicate. Nor do books cover this subject particularly well. Books on CEO leadership tend to either generalise or lionise, with the texture of day-to-day activities and feelings largely missing.

So he proposed that a film crew follow me for a number of weeks to document the life of a CEO. To use a lunar analogy, most people only see one side of a CEO's role: the bright side — the producer wanted to illuminate the unseen dark side!

Why me? First, I had been a CEO for a number of years and had well-established patterns and ways of working. Second, he believed that given my prior academic background I would be sympathetic to the request. I was, but it was still impossible to agree to.

CEOs and, I would suspect, many senior managers have to work in private most of the time — confining them to the dark side, so to speak. Discussions with colleagues about decisions that may or may not be taken, speculation on possible courses of action, negotiations to buy or sell assets or raise money, or reviews of individuals and business units must be uninhibited by the possibility of being reported. As Fairfax is a public company with thousands of shareholders, making these discussions public would have triggered further disclosure requirements from the corporate regulator. Developing and reviewing options and planning would have become impossible.

However, I believed the producer's idea was a good one, and that he had identified an area worth describing and exploring. Consequently, when I finished my work at Fairfax at the end of 2005, I decided to capture the experience of being a CEO in this book. I hope it will be helpful to those seeking to understand the role and to learn and improve as managers and leaders.

I tried to write the book as if I was talking with you and telling you a series of tales about what I found, thought, did and learned from both successes and mistakes, and what it takes to achieve sustained success. To this end I asked Barbara Drury, an experienced journalist and writer, to help. The stories give a texture and reality to my experience that the often sterile and over-generalised language of many management books cannot. They may not be entirely accurate in every detail, as I did not keep diaries, but the stories are my best recollection. I did consider keeping a diary when I started what on some days I thought of as my grandest experiment, but the job of chief executive, particularly in a troubled company, is not just a day job. During the seven years I spent at Fairfax I had no time for writing anything other than the occasional opinion piece for newspapers.

There are many people to thank: my family for putting up with me working on yet another book; my colleagues at Fairfax; the people at the University of New South Wales who helped with the research and preparing the manuscript; and Barbara Drury for her effective and efficient collaboration and assistance. Finally, although this is not an academic text with extensive references, I am indebted to the many scholars whose work I read, used and taught over the years, and whose ideas are reflected in this work.

As a CEO I learned that whatever happened, the responsibility rested with me. It is no different with this book.

Fred Hilmer
January 2007

Introduction

On becoming a rat

It was with some trepidation that I settled on the title of this introduction, 'On becoming a rat', but I did choose it carefully. Few people like rats — they are seen as dirty, aggressive and greedy. Yet they have important uses as subjects of medical and scientific experiments, which make a great contribution to human wellbeing. Occasionally, rat-like behaviour is applauded. Rats have a talent for digging in and surviving against all odds, as Australian troops did when they dug into their desert trenches during the eight-month siege of Tobruk in 1941. To the Germans they were rats in a trap, but Australia's 'Rats of Tobruk' wore the name as a badge of honour. It was these positive aspects of the rat that inspired the title of this introduction.

For most of my working life, until I reached my early fifties, I studied, taught, wrote about or advised on management, strategy and leadership. For most of the 1980s I was the managing director of the Australian practice of McKinsey & Co. For most of the 1990s I served as the dean and professor of management at the Australian Graduate School of Management at the University of New South Wales.

Then, in mid 1998, while teaching a strategy course at the Australian Graduate School of Management, I was phoned by Brian Powers, the newly appointed chair of John Fairfax Holdings Ltd. Although Fairfax is a leading newspaper, magazine and digital publisher, it was not performing well and was in some degree of turmoil. Brian said he needed to see me urgently but didn't say why. I agreed to meet him at the end of the day after I finished teaching. My first thought was that he would ask me to join the board of Fairfax as I had served on a number of boards, including during turnaround situations, such as at Foster's Group from 1990 to 1999.

Brian didn't waste much time getting to the point. (One of his favourite sayings, which he attributes to the late Kerry Packer, is 'subtlety is way overrated!') The reason for the urgent meeting was to ask if I would consider becoming chief executive of Fairfax. The board must have been pretty desperate, as I was hardly a conventional candidate — I had no experience leading a major, publicly owned company and no knowledge of publishing or media. But after three chief executives in three years, the board wanted to try something unconventional.

I decided to take the job for two main reasons. First, it was a great challenge, and after sitting on the sidelines advising and lecturing, I found it hard to resist 'doing'. Second, Fairfax is the most significant source of private independent quality journalism in Australia. Restoring it to good health was worth doing, especially given the critical role of quality journalism in a democracy and market economy. I would have the opportunity, whatever the outcome, to learn about and study management from the inside. If the outcome stabilised Fairfax and put it back on a solid business footing while maintaining its journalistic traditions, then I would have made a contribution I could feel good about.

I am the first to admit the transition from audience to actor was not easy. Fairfax was a troubled company in a cut-throat industry, and the office of chief executive had been weakened by the high turnover of incumbents. When I joined the company I was seen as such an odd choice that there was suspicion in some quarters that I was a puppet for Kerry Packer. Packer had aspired to buy Fairfax but was prevented from doing so by cross-media ownership laws as he controlled a television network. The idea was that Packer would act through his previous associate, Fairfax chair, Brian Powers. However, if there was any question of my independence

When I joined the company I was seen as such an odd choice that there was suspicion in some quarters that I was a puppet for Kerry Packer

it was answered at the first Fairfax Christmas party I hosted in December 1998, barely two months after my arrival. The party was interrupted by security announcing a man delivering a writ from Kerry Packer, directed at me personally for a story in *The Sydney Morning Herald* (the *Herald*). This put everyone beyond doubt that I was my own person.

When scientists need subjects for experiments or study they often use rats. But for management research, rats aren't all that useful. What academics tend to do is study managers in real-life situations, via case studies, surveys or detailed observations. For me, managers were the equivalent of lab rats—so by accepting the Fairfax job I was becoming a rat!

This book is about that experience and, in particular, what it taught me about my central area of interest—what it takes for leaders of large organisations to achieve sustained success.

This is not, however, a book outlining yet another generic success formula. Rather, it concentrates on the key aspects of management

I believe are underemphasised in writing, teaching and discussions of management, but which I found to be critical in my role as chief executive. It was only by becoming a rat that I fully appreciated the importance and difficulty of these underrepresented and often unobserved aspects of management.

The story is told in seven chapters:

1   'An off-the-wall appointment': This chapter describes the Fairfax I walked into in October 1998. It outlines the views of important stakeholders, both inside and outside the company, about what needed to be done to turn the company around and my own assessment of seven serious problems that needed to be tackled.

2   'The success Holy Grail': How to achieve sustained success is the Holy Grail of management because sustained success is both rare and highly rewarding for shareholders and executives. But I call it the Holy Grail for another reason—we haven't found it yet, and not for want of trying. Nevertheless, the search for the Holy Grail has revealed several important, well-developed general ideas about what it takes to succeed. Given my background in teaching and consulting, these ideas were my starting point for tackling the Fairfax challenge.

3   'The Fairfax experience': What I ended up having to do was quite different to the general ideas about what successful companies do. Therefore, in this chapter I outline my Fairfax experience to provide a context for lessons learned. I describe what I did, what happened and what remained to be done when I handed the baton to my successor.

4   'In the hot seat: the decision environment': To further develop the context from which lessons are drawn, this chapter looks at the day-to-day challenges I and, I believe, all chief executives face when making decisions. I discuss time pressure, incomplete information, judgement and the emotional capital we all have tied up in the game.

5   'The positive bias': Although I found no single key to success, a theme did emerge. The main lesson I took away from the experience of being CEO was that the less well-known and often most difficult part of management involves its negative aspects—saying no, disciplining, selling, scaling back, firing and doing without while still achieving targets. Why this is the case and how I dealt with the bias towards positive actions and decisions and against negative ones is the subject of this chapter.

6   'Being positive about negatives': Writing about these negative aspects of management, and how they might better be handled, brought up another side to the book. Effective managers must, at times, be prepared to do things that may cause others to characterise them as 'rats' or as coming from the dark side. But although these negative aspects cannot be avoided by successful managers, they can be handled in a non–rat-like way.

7   'Lessons for leaders and educators': The last chapter discusses leadership and the attributes I believe make a successful leader stand out from the crowd. Although the success of chief executives is most often measured by their corporate results, in my observation it is the measure of the man or the woman that makes the difference between success, failure or mediocrity. Attributes such as brains, energy, determination, trust and ethics are at the heart of management success. Some characteristics of successful leaders are innate, but many can be honed and developed by management education.

The book concludes with a postscript on cross-media ownership laws in Australia—how the legislation affected the media industry and my position during my time at Fairfax, my involvement in seeking statutory changes and my perspective on the potential consequences of recent amendments to the laws.

Much of what I learned is not new. But in my view the day-to-day demands and issues a chief executive of a large public company faces are not well understood. By illuminating this subject with real stories I intend to help practising and would-be managers in both public and private organisations. The stories are less about strategy and organisation structure than about the day-to-day, often unwritten parts of being a chief executive, such as how I handled firing people; how I dealt with negative press, especially from Fairfax's competitors; why I sold the Fairfax art collection; how I misjudged the way Murdoch's News Ltd would compete; how I tackled high costs; and how I organised my time and my interactions with the people who worked with me, inside and outside Fairfax.

I recognise there will be two distinct groups of readers who may approach the book in different ways. Those who are interested in the Australian media industry and Fairfax in particular may be most interested in chapters 1 and 3. However, I suspect the larger body of readers will be most interested in gleaning the lessons I learned at Fairfax and applying them to their own management careers. They will find a summary of management theories of success in chapter 2 and the lessons I learned on the job in the latter half of the book the most useful.

I see myself as a fixer and builder ... I don't like dismantling or retrenching

As this is a personal account, I should start with my own values and biases. First, I see myself as a fixer and builder. That's what I did at McKinsey & Co., the Australian Graduate School of Management and Fairfax—and it's what I intend to do now at the University of New South Wales. I don't like dismantling or retrenching. That may explain why I found tackling negatives—including selling, firing and closing—harder than dealing with positives—such as buying a new business and hiring—but I do not believe I am alone in this respect.

Second, I love learning; I enjoy coming into a new area and trying to figure it out, modelling it in my mind and on paper so that I understand cause and effect. I have been lucky to occupy four major leadership roles so far. Each role has involved leading talented people—consultants, academics, journalists and business people—but each position was quite different. That I didn't know much about media and would have to learn was an important attraction of the Fairfax job.

Third, I presume that people I am dealing with are acting in good faith. Some may call this naïve, and it was an assumption sorely tested in the media, but it generally served me well, particularly when interacting with and developing staff. Media in Australia is, as the book shows, quite a dysfunctional industry, with powerful personalities reacting strongly whenever they feel their egos are threatened. The industry receives media coverage that is out of all proportion to its economic importance. Indeed, media proprietors seem more affected by negative press than non-media owners do. I had more complaints about Fairfax coverage from the other media proprietors than I did from any other group, including politicians!

Finally, I have a low tolerance for politics in an organisation. The right questions are 'What is in the best interests of the organisation?' or 'What are the facts?' The wrong questions are 'What is Sue after?' or 'Can you do this to James, as he is close to the chair?' Fairfax was unusually political, partly because of its journalistic culture and partly because of the turmoil in leadership and ownership. A related problem was people spending time trying to figure out what I wanted to do, when I needed their help in figuring out what we should do. In political organisations the perceived wishes of people in powerful positions are given inordinate and inappropriate weight.

Although I had my share of failures, the overall result was reasonable. The value of Fairfax roughly doubled over my seven years, and total returns to shareholders, dividends and capital gains averaged 9 per cent a year. Most importantly, the company had seven years of stability and independence during which it could continue its main function of being a feisty, independent voice in our democracy.

One of the things I often reflected on was what a chief executive does. Much earlier, in one of my previous jobs, I took one of our daughters to work when my wife was unwell. My daughter sat at a little table and happily entertained herself while I worked. As we drove home she said to me, 'Daddy, now I know what you do: you drink coffee and talk to people all day!'

My point is that as chief executive I didn't make anything, sell papers or advertisements, deliver goods or even collect money — but I did get an appreciation of what is critical. The first and foremost task of a chief executive is selecting a team and then guiding and motivating it. When chief executives change rapidly, poor appointments are made and they're often not fixed, resulting in inconsistent business direction and missed or mishandled opportunities.

Woody Allen is credited with saying that 90 per cent of success is showing up. Staying seven years, providing consistency in direction and values, establishing proper processes and being disciplined about decisions and investments are the less glamorous but probably most critical parts of the job. What's more, you don't have to be a rat, and you can even have fun.

They say cats have nine lives and [Hilmer's] the ninth top Fairfax cat since Warwick Fairfax's tumultuous attempted buy-out left the publisher in a semi-permanent state of executive turnover. He's the second in the procession to have little or no media experience. Bob Mansfield, like Hilmer a company director and businessman, lasted just five months.

Errol Simper
The Weekend Australian
10 October 1998

Chapter 1

An off-the-wall appointment

You can tell a lot about a company by its hiring practices, and in October 1998 newspaper publisher John Fairfax was suffering from an acute siege mentality. Bob Muscat, the group's third chief executive in as many years, had resigned in August 1998 and the board had run out of options. Brian Powers, an American investment banker who had previously worked for Kerry Packer in Australia and Jardine Matheson in Hong Kong, had taken over the reins as chair and started a formal executive search that was going nowhere. Costs were rising faster than revenues and the share price was at best stagnant. In the end someone on the board suggested that each director write down three names that were a bit off-the-wall, people who hadn't been previously considered for the job. My name was the common link between most of their lists.

Against this background my appointment was handled more like an undercover operation than an executive search. On the day of my formal appointment to the top job I was told to meet legal counsel Gail Hambly outside the Fairfax offices, which were at the top of a new tower building overlooking Sydney's Darling Harbour. She escorted me to the basement and up an express lift to the executive floor. In a building full of journalists the board was worried news of my appointment would leak. I was such a controversial choice they wanted to be able to present it as a fait accompli, as if to say, 'here it is, live with it'.

When Brian asked if I would be interested in the job my first reaction was why me? He said that, quite simply, the board's previous more traditional choices had not been successful. Having an industrial manager in the position, like Bob Mansfield, who came from the telecom company Optus, didn't work out. Conversely, Bob Muscat came from a publishing background at Rupert Murdoch's News Ltd, but that hadn't stopped him walking from what was quite a different culture and a tough environment. Attracting high-quality publishing executives to Australia from overseas was difficult and not necessarily successful, as demonstrated by South African newspaper executive Stephen Mulholland's not working out. In the small, inward-looking Australian media market, the most obvious poaching ground was News Ltd, but Murdoch's top executives would not have wanted to come to a dysfunctional Fairfax or stay long term, as had been the case with Bob Muscat. In addition, after years of fractured leadership there were no internal candidates groomed and ready to assume the top job.

The second reason Powers gave was that, even though I had no experience running a public company, I had successfully managed academics at the Australian Graduate School of Management and a group of highly trained professionals at McKinsey & Co. In other words, the board thought I had worked with people similar to those who formed the largest part of its workforce, bright people loyal to their craft rather than the company.

I went away and spoke to friends and colleagues, who warned that the job was a poisoned chalice. From the outside Fairfax was a venerable institution with a history stretching back to the 1830s and some great mastheads. *The Sydney Morning Herald*, *The Age* and *The Australian Financial Review* (*AFR*) are world-class newspapers with a status and political influence that transferred onto the chief executive. I could place a call to the Prime Minister and be confident that he would return it, a privilege not widely available even to top executives. Yet this glittering façade was tainted by a deeply flawed business model and an unstable ownership structure. Major changes in ownership over the decade leading up to my appointment meant the company had neither a consistent board to guide it, nor a consistent chief executive to lead it. The average tenure for chief executives over the decade was one year!

This glittering façade was tainted by a deeply flawed business model and an unstable ownership structure

Despite misgivings, I went back to my three main criteria for doing a job—is it worth doing, will it be fun and is it fairly remunerated? Fairfax is a business that includes a public-interest responsibility, often referred to as a 'public trust'. I strongly believe that intangible infrastructure, such as universities and independent media organisations, are as important as roads and power stations. Fairfax plays an important role in our society and Australia would be the poorer without a commercially sound Fairfax. So clearly I thought the job was worth doing. Would it be fun? Like most people, media was an important part of my life and it seemed an interesting industry to be in. I also enjoy writing and have written my share of opinion pieces for the daily press, so I could identify with the business.

Finally, I spoke at length with senior Fairfax executives and editors. At the end of our discussions I asked them if I should come on board, because I needed to know if I had their support. I think they liked that I was bringing some intellectual rigour to what was seen as a troubled company and that I was not a hired gun employed to cut costs and implement a quick-fix textbook solution.

As for the money, I started on a contract similar to that of my predecessor, Bob Muscat, and left with a termination payment commensurate with industry practice.

First impressions

An overwhelming sense of history and status hit me the first time I walked down the corridor to my new office on the Fairfax executive floor.

The corridor was lined with Fairfax family portraits and big-name, second-tier paintings by Australian artists collected over more than 140 years of the family's control. The only great painting in the collection was Russell Drysdale's 1945 depiction of drought, *Deserted Out-station*, and the rest of the collection was no longer cutting edge. If there is a company tradition of producing quality newspapers and magazines, it should be celebrated by showcasing the group's artists, photographers and journalists — not the collection of paintings bought by owners who had lost the business.

Despite moving from old premises atop a printing press to a prestigious new address, Fairfax had built a formal and traditional office for its chief executive. It was dominated by heavy wooden furniture and big puffy couches; but for me an office is a place of work, not a lounge room. All the major daily newspapers published by Fairfax and News Ltd were displayed, but I was struck by the lack of a bookcase or books. You had to walk through two doors and past a personal assistant's office to enter — hardly an inviting environment. The design insinuated that 'this is the chief executive's office and you don't just wander in'.

The image I would have preferred to project was more like that of *The Washington Post*, where the executive offices were similar to those on the editorial floor, glass-walled and conducive to teamwork. I considered remodelling but I knew that wouldn't go down well with staff while the company was on a savings drive; I could always think of better ways to spend the $1 million or so a new executive area would cost.

Once I had been spirited inside the office Brian Powers asked if I would like a sandwich for lunch. A staff waiter duly arrived in black livery with a silver tray — and this in a company recruiting me to take tens of millions out of the cost base! The whole experience was really incongruous.

These first impressions of a glorious past were at odds with the present state of the business; the Fairfax I inherited was a much diminished company. After emerging from receivership in 1992 in the aftermath of young Warwick Fairfax's failed 1987 buyout, all that was left was the rump of a potentially great media empire. Essentially, a newspaper company with two great metropolitan broadsheets, or what I refer to as the metros, remained. By 1998 the *Herald* and *The Age* accounted for 74 per cent of group revenues and an even greater percentage of profits.

The Australian Financial Review was an exciting business with good potential, but it was tiny. Even with business magazines included, the Business Media division contributed only 12 per cent of revenues. Regional and community newspapers contributed another 12 per cent and other interests barely 2 per cent of revenues. Newspapers in Newcastle and the Illawarra, which protected the *Herald* north and south of Sydney, and in Warrnambool, west of Melbourne, were all Fairfax had been able to keep of rural media. Fairfax also owned some fine suburban newspapers, but they were in the wrong places for the company, in parts of Sydney and Melbourne where people mainly read tabloids rather than the *Herald* or *The Age*. This meant there were few synergies between the metro and suburban papers. Fairfax didn't own the local papers that would have been most valuable to it.

Arguably, some of the wrong businesses had been sold — the Seven television network, the Macquarie radio network and regional papers that formed the foundation of what became Rural Press

Ltd were gone. The only medium Fairfax didn't own prior to its collapse was payTV and you could argue that it would have had a shot at that given its portfolio. The share price graphs in appendix A reinforce the view that Fairfax sold the very parts of the business with the most growth potential.

Years of management uncertainty followed, resulting in a lack of focus or a coherent strategy. This lack of direction was exacerbated by destabilising takeover speculation as shareholders Kerry Packer, Conrad Black and Ron Brierley positioned themselves for a tilt at ownership. When I took up my new post as chief executive, Conrad Black's Hollinger Group of Canada and Ron Brierley's Brierley Investments had been consecutive owners of a 25 per cent block of Fairfax shares, while Kerry Packer's Australian Consolidated Press Holdings held a 15 per cent stake.

One of my first acts as chief executive was to engineer a partial share buyback and placement. The Keating government had indicated it would not allow foreign investors to buy more than 25 per cent, forcing Brierley to accept he was not going to gain control of the company. In early 1999 he offered up his 25 per cent stake, which gave Fairfax an opportunity to stabilise the share register. The company bought back a 10 per cent block of shares and placed the remaining 15 per cent with institutional shareholders at $3.10 a share (compared with a market price of around $3.25 at the time).

In 1998 the composition of the board reflected its chequered history. In his role as partner in US-based private investment firm Hellman & Friedman, chair Brian Powers had been part of the bidding consortium led by Conrad Black, which had also included Kerry Packer for a time. Deputy chair Jonathan Pinshaw was appointed by Brierley Investments but stayed on after he quit the share register.

Seven deadly problems

After a decade of instability Fairfax was a company in urgent need of stable management and renewed focus and direction. My job as chief executive was to chart a course for the next five years and beyond, but from the outset there were different views on the route I should take.

The prevailing view of the board and the market was that a focus on costs should be my top priority. My own view was that cutting costs was a necessary part of the solution but not sufficient to stop the rot. I believed costs were only one of seven deadly problems poisoning Fairfax and hindering its future growth potential. Equally as troubling were the group's loss of market share, unwieldy and ineffective organisational structure, poor management processes and information systems, a strong but

From the outset there were different views on the route I should take

dysfunctional culture and inadequate physical infrastructure. The common link between all these issues, however, was Fairfax's most pervasive problem: the lack of a coherent strategy for growth.

The view from the top

The board believed the company's problems would be solved by cutting costs, improving the journalism and working out how to deal with the digital challenge. The board members saw in me someone who could communicate with journalists and they wanted me to spend more time talking to them. I think some on the board still think that improving the journalism would have helped the company turn a corner, but I never thought it was the key to solving the business challenge. I would have considered focusing on and fixing journalism if the standard was terrible and readers were turning away, but there was little evidence that this was the case.

In my view, the key to improving the business was to work on the things that most needed fixing. If I had to choose between fixing the cost base, fixing the revenue side and evaluating new areas or, on the other hand, improving on journalism that was fundamentally sound, then it was obvious to me where the leverage was.

One board member was adamant that I spend half a day a week in story reviews with journalists, pushing them on the credibility of their sources, why they wrote what they did, whether it was accurate and if there was a better way for them to make their points. That might have been fun but it would have diverted me from the real issues and set a dangerous precedent. I felt quite strongly that the tradition of independent journalism was in the company's best interests and worth preserving. I did raise factual errors when they were brought to my attention but if I had advised journalists on whom or what they could write about it would have been demotivating for them and difficult for me to draw the line. Over the years, both the Murdoch and Packer clans pressured me to clamp down on Fairfax journalists' stories about them. I did not concede. After all, once you stop bad press about one business or person, how do you know who else you should shield from public scrutiny? And how is this in the interests of readers?

The view from the sidelines

When Fairfax came out of receivership in 1992, after a four-and-a-half year absence from the stock market, its shares made their debut on 8 May at $1.20. Within eighteen months the shares had risen to $3.00, where they stayed locked in a tight trading range between $2.50 and $3.50 for the best part of six years. Before joining the company I made a bet with a friend who thought the share price would rise when my appointment was announced because it would end the uncertainty. I won the bet because the shares fell, but they only fell by $0.03 before soon recovering, which underlines the futility of placing too much emphasis on short-term share price movements.

The first people I visited on assuming the chief executive's role were stockbrokers, analysts and institutional shareholders. For the most part they didn't share my view that the business was vulnerable. They agreed with the board that Fairfax had a fabulous franchise it was not milking enough and that it could ride out the competitive threats without diversifying. Their message to me was to cut costs because they were rising faster than revenues.

Tellingly, the most astute observer of Fairfax was the late Kerry Packer, then still firmly at the helm of Publishing and Broadcasting Ltd. Not long after I started at Fairfax Brian Powers said Kerry Packer would like to have lunch with me but wouldn't suggest it in case I declined. Brian added that if I were to call him, however, and propose lunch then Packer would invite me to his office.

After this delicate toing and froing I met Packer for an illuminating lunch at his Park Street headquarters. I stayed until 5.00 pm because I soon realised he knew the Fairfax business better than anyone else I had spoken to, including the board. He knew it in great detail, down to the rough turnover and margins of each of the regional papers. He didn't talk much about editorial, although he was clearly irritated by some of the comments about the Packer family. Instead he talked about Fairfax as a business, the threats to classifieds and the need to be ruthless about costs. I asked him why he was interested in the business if the problems were as bad as he said they were, to which he replied, 'I'm a rich man. Think of it as an indulgence'. I learned later that he'd had McKinsey & Co. do a study of the classified business at Fairfax. It was clearly a business he had looked at very closely.

....

The initial market verdict was scathing, with analysts claiming the appointment was misguided and a complete surprise. 'The market will see this as a negative', one analyst said, while another claimed Fairfax must have found no other more suitable candidates.

Peter Witts, *The Weekend Australian*, 10 October 1998

....

A flawed strategy

In a well-run company there is a live agenda of development opportunities that operates something like a news list, the set of possible stories for tomorrow's paper. This means you can be confident the company is going to grow because management is continually looking at growth opportunities. Fairfax had no list of growth options and no coherent strategy.

I'm a great believer in the notion that companies without a coherent strategy will fail and that maintaining a competitive edge is crucial to any strategy. As Nobel prize–winning economist George Stigler wrote, a competitive market is a tough weed that quickly overruns an uncompetitive company.

Fairfax had a competitive edge ... but it was undergoing death by a thousand cuts as every aspect of its advantage was being eroded

Fairfax had a competitive edge in its great newspaper franchises and large-scale printing presses, but it was undergoing death by a thousand cuts as every aspect of its advantage was being eroded. The metropolitan broadsheets were no longer a unique source of classifieds and were fast losing their special status as news providers. Fairfax had great brands, but an increasing number of younger readers were moving away from them to log on or tune out. Technological improvements meant the company no longer had the exclusive ability to print a metropolitan daily; there were smaller printing plants in Sydney that could print competitive content.

The problem facing metropolitan newspapers is essentially the same one encountered by department stores. Department stores are facing a tough slog everywhere because almost everything they do can be done better by a specialist retailer. No-one else did general news in Sydney or Melbourne as well as the *Herald* and *The Age*, but there were many specialist providers chipping away at the motoring, real estate, business, employment and sport sections of the paper. If I want golf results or statistics, as I often do, I can find them much more readily and in more depth on specialist internet sites than in my daily paper.

This produces a dilemma: how to build a competitive advantage in a declining industry while keeping your attackers at bay. Although there was recognition at Fairfax that the internet was coming, it was overemphasised at the expense of more sensible, repairable problems.

The classic business strategy in a mature industry is to consolidate and rationalise—to shore up the advantages you already have through mergers, acquisitions and strategic asset sales. To this end, the automobile and airline industries have undergone more than a decade of takeover activity. In newer industries, such as software or the internet, early fragmentation gives way to consolidation as the industry matures and companies seek cost advantages in greater economies of scale. These are classic strategies but they are no help if the real cause of decline is not acknowledged.

The Washington Post Company is a good example of a quality newspaper company that saw the writing on the wall. It has remained one of the world's most profitable media concerns by diversifying into education and broadcasting, thereby reducing its core newspaper asset to about 20 per cent of its business. When I visited its chief executive, Donald Graham, early in my tenure he made this observation: 'The Washington paper is at the core of our values but it is not the core of our business any more because it's not a business that has the growth our shareholders expect. The Washington Post Company is not *The Washington Post* paper or we would be out of business'.

By comparison, The New York Times Company can't get its mind off its flagship newspaper, and total shareholder returns from its share price plus dividends went backwards during my seven years at Fairfax from 1998 to 2005 (for a comparison of the annualised total returns of international newspapers during this period, see appendix B). Knight Ridder, Tribune and Gannett are also premier US newspaper companies who have stuck to their knitting and managed costs well, but whose total shareholder returns have stalled at below 5 per cent.

London's Daily Mail has been more successful. Although it is a good operator loyal to its core business, it is also a tabloid newspaper company and, hence, unlike Fairfax, driven more by display advertisements than classifieds. Even so, total shareholder returns from the Daily Mail and Fairfax were level pegging at 9 per cent a year during the period, while The Washington Post Company managed an even more respectable 13 per cent total return per annum. In stark contrast to the challenges facing metropolitan broadsheets, the star performer during this period was the British regional newspaper group Johnston Press, with a total shareholder return of 18 per cent per annum. In Australia, papers with regional monopolies, such as at West Australian News and Rural Press Ltd, were also strong performers.

There was a widespread belief at Fairfax that readers would return to the fold if editorial content was improved. If editorial content is of poor quality and nobody else has a competitive advantage in printing or classifieds, then you could work on restoring editorial credibility. However, it is a questionable strategy if the world has moved on through no fault of your own and the business is being chipped away by competitors.

An alternative was for Fairfax to consolidate by buying more regional and suburban newspapers. This is the strategy suggested by *New York Times* journalist Thomas Friedman in his book *The Lexus and the Olive Tree*. He makes the point that if you can't make a world-beating product like the Lexus there is always a role for 'olive trees'—local products that give people comfort and a voice in a globalising world. Local and regional papers are olive trees and potentially very profitable ones, as Rural Press Ltd in Australia and Johnston Press in the UK have shown.

Another alternative was to use the company's own market insight to buy a competitive advantage that someone else was not fully exploiting. Fairfax's purchase of the INL publishing business in New Zealand from News Ltd is a neat example of this, which I describe in detail in chapter 3. A third strategy open to Fairfax was to move into adjacent high-growth areas that contain some risk. For Kerry Packer's Publishing and Broadcasting Ltd this meant investing in the internet, gambling and casinos, while Rupert Murdoch's News Ltd moved into payTV, movies, television and the internet.

Immediately before taking on the job at Fairfax I had been deputy chair of the Foster's Group. There I saw how a single-product company based on a mature product, beer, must diversify geographically and by line of business to keep growing. Since Foster's Group made a major acquisition in wine with the purchase of Mildura Blass and, most recently, Southcorp, the company has continued to grow and prosper.

The Fairfax situation was similar to the challenge facing Foster's Group and many other mature, single-product companies; however, Fairfax lacked a strategy or at best was pursuing a flawed one. The board's favoured route of cutting costs, improving editorial and trying to figure out what the internet might mean, ran counter to a classic mature-industry strategy of consolidation, rationalisation and sensible gambles on new businesses.

Eroding market share

Fairfax had an enviable newspaper franchise with a deserved reputation for strong independent journalism and dedicated readers. Although this resulted in pricing power in the market, the source of revenue that leveraged the company's business model was under threat.

All the cash at Fairfax flowed from the car, real estate and employment classifieds—the prized rivers of gold—but by 1998 the market's focus was shifting to the internet. In the heady atmosphere of the dotcom boom the board had been spooked by a report out of the US by Forrester Research saying newspapers would lose significant amounts of classified advertising revenue by 2005.

In fact, the immediate threat was not from the internet but from specialist publications such as the *Trading Post* and community newspapers that dominated certain classified categories. They were able to sit under the Fairfax price umbrella and charge less for advertisements because they had little or no editorial cost, or space devoted to editorial content. Former Fairfax journalist and editor Eric Beecher saw where large profits were being made and bought into community newspapers in 1990 with his Text Media Group, before selling the business to Fairfax in 2004 for $60 million.

At the same time, the audience for newspapers was fragmenting, and circulations were edging downwards at about 1 per cent per annum, a trend experienced by major metropolitan broadsheets worldwide. Only a small percentage of young people were reading newspapers for news and entertainment, and other readers were also using alternative media sources. The company's response to this phenomenon of aging readers and a loss of classified volumes and listings was to raise advertising rates by 6 to 8 per cent each year and to lift cover prices by about 10 per cent annually.

The loss of market share was also masked by poor measurement. Fairfax measured market share in a number of ways, but it mostly resorted to a comparison between Fairfax and News Ltd. If the company wanted to find its share of the Sydney employment-advertisement market, someone would add up column centimetres of job advertisements in the *Herald* and compare this with News Ltd's *The Daily Telegraph*. By contrast, the internet, suburban and specialist publications were ignored, and the information that was collected was either incomplete or misleading.

When I served on the Coca-Cola Amatil board one of the things its directors talked about was 'share of stomach'. Traditionally, Coca-Cola Amatil had measured its share of the cola market against arch rival Pepsi until someone suggested the statistics be reframed to determine Coke's share of the broader beverage market. These days if someone buys a cup of coffee or juice, or drinks a free glass of water, Coca-Cola Amatil wants to know why he or she is not buying one of its drinks. This approach has led the company to market more aggressively and introduce a successful range of new products.

If you are in a mature industry that is losing market share in key categories, as Fairfax was, you will continue to believe you are doing well if you only compare yourself with companies that are facing similar challenges, like News Ltd. Meanwhile, a niche player like the *Trading Post* or suburban newspapers had more of some types of ads than both News Ltd and Fairfax combined—but the company did not recognise them as competitors.

I underestimated the degree of attachment people had to the newspaper business, from the boardroom down to the editorial floor

Many companies reach a stage where they have to change their business when it reaches maturity or faces new competition. I didn't think Fairfax had an insurmountable problem, but I underestimated the degree of attachment people had to the newspaper business, from the boardroom down to the editorial floor.

A favourite saying of Greg Hywood, former publisher of *The Age* and the *Herald*, was 'If we build it they will come', taken from the American baseball film *Field of Dreams*. Incorporating this concept into its business strategy was the mistake made by Harley-Davidson when its iconic status among the motorcycle fraternity was challenged by Honda. Harley-Davidson traditionally dominated the bigger and more expensive end of the market and regarded Japanese motorcycles as cheap, inferior and lacking in grunt. Then, in the 1970s, when Honda's quality and performance improved and it began to build bigger and more powerful bikes, Harley-Davidson embarked on a period of cost cutting. The strategy left Harley-Davidson with expensive bikes that were inferior in performance, quality and handling compared with its Japanese counterparts. Harley-Davidson believed its brand name would ensure customer loyalty and that it could keep ahead of the competition by raising prices from an unassailable position at the quality end of the market—a strategy that almost sent it to the wall.

There are similarities between the Harley-Davidson experience and Fairfax's reliance on raising prices to compensate for its falling market share. After a change in ownership Harley-Davidson re-established its competitive edge by building on the appeal of its classic 'hogs' and improving attention to technological innovation.

Rising costs of people and paper

The impact of declining market share on Fairfax's profits was exacerbated by poor cost controls. The company's two single biggest costs were people and paper, with staff accounting for 42 per cent of all costs in 1998 and newsprint and paper another 21 per cent. Both areas used long-term contractual arrangements that were not sustainable.

One glaring example was the enterprise-bargaining agreement with journalists. It included cost-of-living adjustments and a profit-share arrangement. Unusually, the profit-share component was first paid as a bonus and then added to the cost-of-living adjustment in the base salary. In other words, profit share was paid not just for the year in which it was earned, but in perpetuity!

As a result, the enterprise-bargaining formula not only caused costs to rise faster than inflation, but it also exacerbated the cyclical nature of the business. When a bad year followed a good one, costs would go up by more than the cost of living because the previous good year's profit share was absorbed into the base. And when a good year followed a bad one, costs would look great because revenue would rise, but wages would only go up by the cost of living adjustment (since there had been no profit share in the bad year). The concept of profit share is founded on it being separate to base salary. I could never understand how the company agreed to an arrangement that locked it into cost rises that were above inflation.

Newsprint was another example of flawed contracts. Fairfax bought its newsprint from an Australian plant in Albury that based its prices on West Coast Paper prices from the US. The contract was renegotiated annually to reflect currency and world paper-price changes, which for the plant and Fairfax meant a boom or bust cycle. Changing to an Australian-dollar contract with caps and collars to limit annual fluctuations due to currency and world price changes saved millions of dollars and provided stability.

Poor management processes

At Fairfax processes were appalling. It is difficult to cut costs in an organisation if nobody knows where the costs are hiding. Yet the company lacked systematic management processes and information systems to track the cost of producing a newspaper, purchasing equipment or managing staff.

There was also no regular cycle of meetings with members of the management team to track progress and work on strategy. This meant people were unclear about what was expected of them and the company was unsure about where it was headed.

Editorial was just one area where there was no analysis of process. For example, the daily editorial cycle begins with a story idea and ends with publication. In a perfect world the story would be written with little need for alteration; but in reality, some stories at Fairfax were touched up to thirty times on the journey to publication. When that is the case you need to know the minimum production cost of a story and the cost at the other extreme—that is, after thirty hands have touched it—and then ask what accounted for the difference in cost. If you don't break the costs down into components you are just guessing.

Some of my most difficult meetings within the company were with the newspaper publishers—not because they were difficult people but because they had little or no experience of management processes within a large public company. The newsprint cost in their accounts would go up and they would be unable to tell me why, or I would ask for a detailed analysis of staff numbers and functions and the figures on their spreadsheet wouldn't add up. They obviously found our weekly meetings difficult too because they jokingly referred to them as the weekly beatings!

Personnel processes were also weak, with no performance reviews or systematic feedback, making it difficult to identify and promote talented people. This stemmed from a long-standing editorial tradition of egalitarianism and collective bargaining where all rewards were shared equally. Hence, pay was not performance or merit based but tied to awards and pay bands. That culture can only exist when a monopoly in classifieds provides a 30 per cent–plus profit margin—enabling you to simply raise your price when earnings are under pressure. It is not a tolerable culture when the business is being threatened and there are high disparities in contribution and in performance.

Ineffective organisational structure

An unwieldy management structure was partly to blame for the weak management processes at Fairfax. At the time of my appointment the role of chief executive was ill defined and had gone through many changes. Below the chief executive in the company hierarchy was a management team of eighteen, but there was no theme to the structure. The management team all reported directly to me, including the editor of the *Good Weekend* magazine, which was distributed with *The Age* and the *Herald* on Saturdays, and the managers of the *Warrnambool Standard*, *Newcastle Herald* and *Illawarra Mercury*, Fairfax's three regional papers.

Although there is a clear trend in business to flatten management structures, with so many people reporting to me it was impossible to establish a good dialogue with each of them. There was also no centralised advertising or sales, internet development had been lumped in with corporate strategy and the mastheads operated like competing fiefdoms. This unwieldy and fractured management structure made it difficult to focus on profit-and-loss targets and to manage and control costs, and it also made it difficult to hold people accountable.

A lack of financial literacy was part of the problem

A lack of financial literacy was part of the problem; many of the costs in a newspaper's profit-and-loss statement are allocated on a basis few publishers understand. Consequently, people at Fairfax did not feel ownership or responsibility for their part of the business. A by-product was that managers tended to delegate operational matters to the chief executive, leaving me little time to work on strategy.

A dysfunctional culture

Remuneration was not the only facet of the business steeped in a culture that was sometimes counterproductive. While a strong journalistic culture is valuable, there were elements of the tradition that were holding back the business. One example was the prevailing sense among editorial staff that the business side of the newspaper industry was the enemy of editorial independence. This made it impossible to work across mastheads to save costs because each publication functioned as a self-contained silo in competition with the others. So if *The Age* had a scoop its editorial staff would refuse to share it with the *Herald* until after publication.

Although competition is healthy, particularly between companies, it made no sense to compete across different metropolitan markets, where the readership is quite separate. It made even less sense to compete in non-news sections of the paper, but that didn't stop journalists mounting some creative arguments. One of the things I grew to love about journalists was their cleverness in pursuit of what they saw as editorial interests. In one instance I was trying to explain the need to copy share to the motoring writers, arguing that a review of the new Toyota or BMW need not be different in Sydney and Melbourne. One journalist insisted you couldn't run an article about a Sydney road test in the Melbourne paper because Sydney was hilly and Melbourne was flat! The reality was that road tests only ever include information about driving on a gravelly surface—and none focuses on the so-called hilliness of Sydney!

Editorial was further divided along hard news and soft news lines. One of the great battles in contemporary journalism is hard news stories and analysis fighting for space with softer stories on lifestyle, celebrities and popular culture. Many journalists and their editors regard soft news as unworthy, even if it is popular with readers. They rail against the 'dumbing down' of quality media in the pursuit of younger readers and those who have little time or inclination for serious, issues-based journalism. The issue of quality journalism resonated with me as someone from an academic background. Getting the right mix between soft and hard news was a great but necessary challenge.

By the time I arrived in 1998 there had already been many years of cost cutting, the introduction of more lifestyle content into the metros and management attempts to move away from collective bargaining. As a result, journalists were cynical about reform and had developed a victim mentality that stifled individual initiative.

Inadequate physical infrastructure

Further down the production chain, the company's two printing plants at Chullora in Sydney and inside the antiquated Age building in Melbourne were facing capacity constraints. My home phone in Sydney would start ringing from 6.30 on Saturday mornings as irate readers and newsagents called to say their papers hadn't been delivered. There were fewer calls from Melbourne, where the problems were worse due to delays caused by even poorer plant, but probably only because it required a costly long-distance phone call.

I put an end to the calls by delisting my phone number; although fixing the problem with the presses took much longer.

Information technology was another area with huge inefficiencies. Newspapers are an information processing business and Fairfax had different computer systems for financial functions and payroll, circulation, editorial, advertisement sales and printing. On top of that there were separate IT departments at *The Age*, the *Herald*, regional and community newspapers and the Chullora printing plant in Sydney. Many of these outdated IT systems needed to connect with each other but they were being replaced piecemeal, often with something completely incompatible. My first inkling that the various IT systems were not talking to each other was when I received my first pay cheque and it was wrong!

The search for solutions

This is the Fairfax I inherited in 1998. At first glance Fairfax was undoubtedly a worthy institution, with a proud tradition of quality newspapers and independent journalism. But this strength was also the company's weakness. Like many companies with a sense of their own history and importance, Fairfax failed to see the vulnerability of its traditional business. Although there was some recognition of the challenges ahead—from the internet and other competing sources of news and information—Fairfax failed to recognise the extent of the problems it faced within its own walls.

As the new chief executive it was my job to fix the problems. Although there was clearly no simple solution that would ensure the company's long-term success, the problems facing Fairfax were not unique (traditional newspaper companies around the world faced similar challenges). But after visiting a number of newspaper companies in the US and Europe I concluded that none offered an antidote that could be readily applied to Fairfax. So as a former academic it was natural for me to turn to management textbooks for guidance.

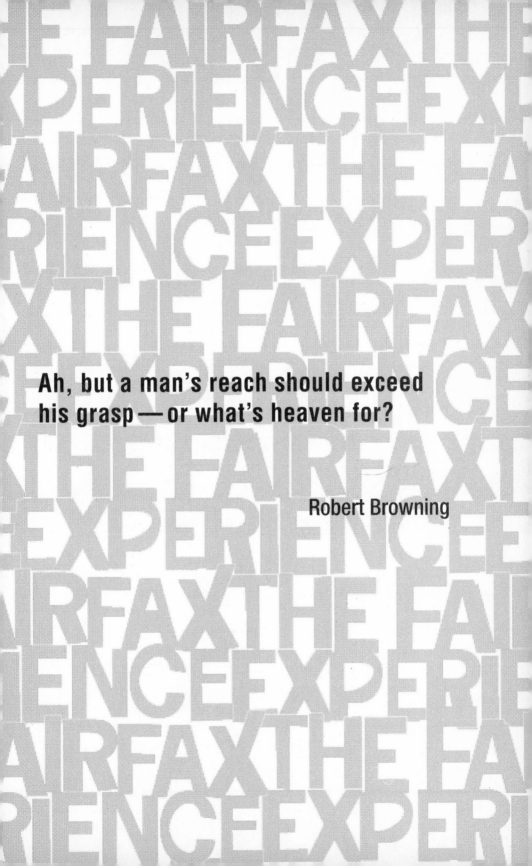

Ah, but a man's reach should exceed
his grasp — or what's heaven for?

Robert Browning

Chapter 2

The success Holy Grail

There is no question that Fairfax had the makings of a great company. Its mastheads and brands were outstanding, and they were supported by loyal readers with the high incomes and education prized by advertisers. The quality of its journalism was high and, despite the turmoil of the late eighties and mid nineties, the staff was dedicated to producing good products. Yet even with these positive attributes Fairfax was in deep trouble. The road to recovery would be long and difficult and by no means assured. Like a sporting team on a losing streak, Fairfax needed to get back into form before it could return to the winner's circle. Or, to borrow from Jim Collins's *Good to Great*, Fairfax needed to learn how to become a good company again before it could aspire to being great.[1]

For Fairfax to become a good company depended on how the board dealt with the seven serious and related problems discussed in chapter 1, namely:

♦ a flawed strategy for growth

- eroding market share masked by price increases and lack of market intelligence and data

- high and escalating costs

- poor management processes and information systems

- an unwieldy and ineffective organisational structure

- a strong but increasingly dysfunctional culture

- inadequate physical infrastructure.

Before tackling these issues I needed to be certain of my goal. I knew what I didn't want—a quick fix or a short-term turnaround. Generally, improving performance for a short time is easy, particularly if there is little concern for the long term. Costs can be cut, prices can be raised, investment activities, such as research or new product development, can be curtailed and short-term results immediately improved. This would have been easy to accomplish at Fairfax because there was potential to cut costs and pursue aggressive pricing; but these types of results are usually ephemeral because they come at the expense of future growth.

Instead I agreed with the board that the goal was to put the company on a sustainable footing that was consistent with its public trust role and tradition as a quality publisher. This had to be achieved while also obtaining satisfactory short-term performance—letting costs escalate further, market share slip and cash flows dry up would have been unacceptable to the large institutional shareholders. In short, the board and shareholders wanted to have it both ways: good results year in and year out (albeit in a highly cyclical industry) while the company also dealt with its seven core problems. I was committed to delivering the outcome they wanted.

There are two reasons that achieving such sustained success is the Holy Grail for practising managers and academics. The first and most obvious is that success brings rewards. All managers want every year to be a good year, if not in an absolute sense then at least relative to their peers. Pay, status, self-esteem and job security all depend on results—and the typical measure of results is returns to shareholders. Whether for a company or an industry group, every shareholder and board member wants good returns and they are prepared to pay management handsomely for it. Second, sustained success by any measure is extremely rare. Few people achieve it, and even those who accomplish it for substantial periods of ten to fifteen years tend to fall back to average or below-average performance.

Due to my background in academia and consultancy, and my continuing interest in what makes successful organisations tick, I started to think about how the Holy Grail might be achieved at Fairfax in light of the following considerations:

- *Sustained success is rare.* Although I was broadly aware of this point I was surprised by how few companies consistently outperformed their peers when I reviewed the statistics on corporate performance in Australia and internationally.

- *The keys to success are well documented.* There are some consistent findings about what it takes to achieve sustained success in terms of strategy, people management, customer relationships and financial discipline. There is also research about approaches that generally don't work, including acquisitions or adoption of the latest fad, such as re-engineering or quality management.

- *Application and theory are entirely different.* The hard part is not in identifying these themes but in applying them to the real-life situations faced by practising managers.

Sustained success is rare

Warren Buffett is the most talked about, studied and emulated investment manager in the world. From humble beginnings he amassed billions of dollars for himself and his shareholders, consistently earning returns above the market average. He did this not by trading stocks but by building up and holding stakes for long periods in companies that went on to perform at above average levels.

Outlined in appendix C, Buffett's approach to identifying these exceptional investments is completely transparent. He describes both his philosophy and the details of his investments in his regular reports to shareholders. His formula for success is also well documented in a number of books, albeit not written by Buffett himself. Yet although many other fund managers try to copy what he does, few manage to outperform the market average, and none approaches his level of long-term performance. Why? Because finding companies that will consistently outperform is extremely hard.

Only a handful of companies out of the thousands available for investment meet Buffett's test. Even then, the process of identifying winning companies before their share prices and dividends take off is beyond the skill of most investors. Buffett gives lots of clues about how he picks his stocks—the types of businesses, the management, the cash flows and the financial ratios—but others using the same guidelines fail to produce the same results.

Sustained success is not just unusual; it is extremely rare

Statistics shed some light on why this is the case. Sustained success is not just unusual; it is extremely rare. A recent study by Alfred Marcus in his book *Big Winners and Big Losers*[2] looked at the 1000 largest US corporations between 1992 and 2002 and reviewed similar studies of earlier periods. The findings are dramatic. Marcus found that:

- 'Many companies perform better than their competitors for short periods of time, but few are able to sustain competitive advantage over a long period'.

- 'Natural parity is the condition that prevails in most industries'. (In other words, most participants in an industry earn similar returns over time, though performance will vary year to year.)

- 'From 1992 to 2002 only about 3 per cent of the 1000 largest US corporations consistently and significantly outperformed their industry's average stock market performance and about 6 per cent did the opposite'.

A similar exercise in Australia supported these results. My colleagues and I compared the performances of sixty-six of the top one hundred companies with an average return for three-year and ten-year periods between 1995 and 2005. We found that:

- Only 20 per cent of companies outperformed the average in any given three-year period between 1995 and 2005. (That is, even with a relatively short three-year horizon you have only a one-in-five chance of doing better than average.)

- Only 6 per cent of companies beat the index in every three year rolling period over the 10 years.

Other studies using slightly different periods and types of measurement produced similar results, finding that only 2 to 5 per cent of companies are consistent winners.

As the bar is raised—resulting in the period for which success is required getting longer or the degree to which the company beats the average becoming greater—even fewer companies are consistent winners. One of the best-known studies of sustained excellence is *Good to Great* by Jim Collins. His criterion for being a great company was cumulative returns at least three times the market average over a period of fifteen years, following fifteen average or below-average years. In other words, he was looking for companies that went from sustained average performance to sustained excellence. From an initial set of the Fortune 500 only eleven companies, or just over 2 per cent, made the grade.

Considering what happens when a company has either a few bad years or a few good years, these aren't surprising results. When a company goes through a bad patch the pressure to improve is intense. Often a new chief executive and top team are brought in, hard decisions are made and the company's performance moves back in line with its industry. When a company has a few good years the high returns are like a magnet to competitors who try to emulate the successful company or leapfrog its practices. When this happens it doesn't take many competitors to erode returns.

In his book *Memoirs of an Unregulated Economist* Nobel Laureate George Stigler describes how margins in bond tenders dropped when only one or two competitors entered the market. When a company wants to sell bonds, it typically calls for tenders from groups of banks, who charge a margin for providing the money and reselling the bond. When twenty groups bid, the margin was about $14 per $1000 bond; when only one group bid it was $20; with two bidders it fell to $17; and with three bidders it fell to $16. In other words, even a single competitor can have a significant impact on your profit margin. Rather than likening competition to a 'delicate flower', Stigler refers to it as a 'tough weed', the effect of which is difficult to avoid.[3]

In the corporate arena competition is intensifying due to both technology and globalisation, but the effects of competition are not restricted to business. In areas as diverse as sport and academia, few teams, individuals or organisations stay on top for more than ten years in a row. As Collins discovered, the best and worst performers tend to revert to average after a few years at the margins.

Yet some companies do achieve sustained success—the big question is how. There is a strong, although perhaps illogical, belief that if the Holy Grail can be found more companies will become the consistent winners their managers and owners want them to be.

The keys to success

The pursuit of lasting success is probably the most widely written about and read about area of management. Almost all the business bestsellers tackle this subject, either by studying sets of companies (such as in *In Search of Excellence, Built to Last, Good to Great, Consistent Winners and Losers, The First XI Winning Organisations of Australia*) or by examining the experience of successful leaders, such as Jack Welch at General Electric (GE), Roberto Goizueta at Coca-Cola Amatil and Frank Lowy at Westfield. All the studies are open to academic criticism. Was the sample big enough? Were the criteria rigorous enough? Were the comparisons appropriate? Did performance fall away almost as soon as the research was completed? These are justifiable questions, and proper subjects for academic discussion and review. However, I found it more helpful as a practising manager to look for some common themes that seemed to make sense and then to see if these themes could be applied.

I found myself facing the same challenge that investment managers do when they try to employ Warren Buffett's method of picking winning stocks. Setting out general rules and principles is easy; making it happen is where life becomes hard but interesting.

If you want to run a successful company over time, four issues stand out: a strong strategic position, effective people management, a customer focus and financial discipline (see appendix D for this composite formula for sustained business success). The only real dispute between different studies of consistent overachievers is over which issues are more important.

Holding the strategic high ground

In order to succeed in business you need what Warren Buffett calls an 'economic moat'. Like a medieval castle perched on high ground, the modern company needs a strategic position protected by a wide moat that makes it hard for competitors to attack. The moat may be a brand name, pricing power or a market monopoly.

Others, such as Michael Porter in his classic book *Competitive Strategy*, use a more elaborate economic framework. According to Porter, if your market is easy to enter and attack and hard to quit, if suppliers and customers are more powerful than you and if you don't have a significant market share, you can't expect to earn good returns.[4]

The airline business is a case in point. Every country wants at least one airline and banks and aircraft manufacturers are happy to finance new players—making the market relatively easy to enter. But once you are in the business it is hard to quit, so companies struggle for years with low returns. Used aircraft is hard to sell without taking large losses and staff redundancy costs are high. The key suppliers—aircraft manufacturers, fuel companies and airports—are more powerful than most airlines. In addition, due to the internet, customers can compare prices assiduously. These factors make sustained success in airlines difficult to achieve unless the company is able to deal with them. So far only a few discount airlines or those with protected routes have been able to do so and generally only for relatively short periods.

To make life even tougher, just having a good strategic position often isn't enough. In competitive markets the high returns earned from a good position are like a flashing neon sign to competitors, who then intensify their efforts to attack your position. To earn sustained returns your spot in the market must be defensible and you must have the will and capability to defend it. For example, Netscape had a good position in internet browsers but it couldn't hold off Microsoft; Apple had a unique position in PCs but it couldn't hold off IBM; and in Australia, Franklins supermarkets had a special cost–price position but it couldn't hold off Woolworths supermarkets.

There was no question that Fairfax had competitive advantages as a result of its strong historic connection with readers and advertisers—but these advantages were eroding. Suburban papers were taking a share of the market for housing advertisements and there were few barriers to stop new suburban papers. At the same time, specialised classified papers like the *Trading Post* or *Nine to Five* started to eat into the market for car and job advertisements. In addition, in the background loomed the internet, which threatened to steal even more of the classifieds market. Ominously, all these competitors could offer prices well below those required to produce news-rich broadsheets with large bands of journalists. For Fairfax, cutting prices would not solve the positioning problem because new competitors could match lower prices, destroying industry profitability.

It's all about people

A second ingredient in the formula for success is people. Pick the right people, motivate and empower them, recognise and reward their achievements, build and reinforce a strong culture and strategy will take care of itself. This is hard to argue with. After all, who wants to have the wrong people? But the dilemma is whether the people side of business is sufficient in itself to produce sustained success. Warren Buffett doesn't think so. As he puts it, 'when a management with a reputation for brilliance tackles a business with a reputation for poor fundamental economics, it is the reputation of the business that stays intact'.[5]

Pick the right people, motivate and empower them, recognise and reward their achievements

Another consideration is whether these general rules are specific enough to be helpful. What makes a person 'right'? When I started at Fairfax there was a strong view that the publisher of a paper has to have an editorial background, without which he or she wouldn't be 'right'. However, I soon found that business acumen, competitive drive, initiative, strength of character and energy were more important, provided the manager understood and appreciated the journalism.

Another example of people-focused business strategy is the supposed effectiveness of 'hoopla', the type of public celebration of success used by the likes of Tupperware and McDonald's to motivate employees. I was far from confident that this approach made sense at Fairfax with its strong culture of editorial independence underpinned by healthy cynicism.

Nevertheless, no study of success says people are unimportant. The processes by which people are hired, targets set, performance feedback given, success celebrated, learning carried out and rewards paid are considered vital. These were areas where Fairfax had more gaps than a solid platform to build on. Despite the evident goodwill of employees towards the company, their pride in its publications and the quality of its independent journalism, the hard edges of performance management were missing.

Courting the customer

The third source of sustained business success is happy customers. Stay close to customers, delight them, treat them as partners and as a source of ideas and never take a customer for granted. This is not just common sense or short-term selling tactics—strong relationships with customers are a source of ongoing competitive advantage. Customers generally incur costs when switching from one supplier to another. They have to find a new supplier, assess whether their needs will be met, negotiate or determine price and establish credit. The less reason they have to switch, the harder it is for a competitor or new supplier to attack your customers. (Consumer service providers, such as banks, telcos and insurers, understand this.) By encouraging customers to bundle products and services in return for discounts and loyalty rewards, inertia will prevent all but the most motivated customers from switching providers.

Serving customers well can also provide a warm inner glow for staff. People in a company are often highly motivated by providing a good product or service and then being thanked and recognised for doing so by customers. Customer satisfaction and recognition is also seen as an objective way to assess the performance and subsequent reward of individuals and departments.

Applying those ideas at Fairfax, however, was not straightforward. There were at least two groups of customers—readers and advertisers—and their interests were not necessarily the same. A reader would expect the front page to set out the most important news stories and give a taste of what is inside the paper, whereas an advertiser may want to see most, if not all, of the front page available for an advertisement. To complicate matters, advertisers usually dealt with the company through agencies and media buyers whose interests were often different. Agencies and media buyers wanted to demonstrate that they could get the best price for their customer; Fairfax, by comparison, wanted the highest price it could achieve for the advertising space.

In addition, a strong editorial culture in a paper of record would at times produce coverage that did not please customers, but which editors strongly felt was their duty to put before a reader. A vivid example was the front page of *The Australian Financial Review* on 11 September 2001, which reported the destruction of the World Trade Center. A large photograph showed bodies falling from the burning towers as people threw themselves off the building in a last desperate act. That morning the phones rang incessantly and the comments were overwhelmingly critical. The editor-in-chief's position was clear—it happened and Fairfax had a duty to show what happened without sugar-coating it. A less graphic example of coverage that doesn't please customers is when stories become more important to journalists than readers, who lose interest in what they see as nothing new.

Despite these difficulties, the customer dimension was one that wasn't receiving enough attention at Fairfax. There was undoubtedly room for improvement.

Financial discipline

The final source of sustained excellence mentioned in business literature is financial discipline. This idea comes from the view that in a large, complex, multiproduct or multibusiness company the crucial role of the top management is to allocate capital. Consistently earning better-than-average shareholder returns requires that every dollar of investment pays at least its cost of capital. It is no good having a wonderful strategic position, even a monopoly, if you over-invest in plant, technology or products that erode the average return. If capital isn't going into areas that earn good returns, then motivated staff or delighted customers is not enough.

The benefit of this approach is that the impact of every decision on shareholder value is made clear both to the manager seeking capital and the manager allocating it—keeping shareholder interests front and centre of management decision making.

If capital isn't going into areas that earn good returns, then motivated staff or delighted customers is not enough

However, it requires a team of financially sophisticated managers to apply the techniques effectively, by producing the right information and being able to interpret and make judgements about it.

As with other approaches, financial discipline may well be necessary, but not sufficient in itself for sustained success. Fairfax, however, was well behind most companies in terms of financial discipline and this was a prospective area that could be improved relatively quickly by tightly centralising capital allocation. All the company needed to do was ensure that significant capital could not be outlayed without the chief financial officer's and my approval—which would only be given when we were confident that rigorous return criteria were likely to be met.

What doesn't work

The flip side of success is failure, and one of the most interesting by-products of studies of success is recognition of what doesn't work. The four principles outlined above were drawn out by researchers who wanted us to learn from other people's successes. However, it is also possible to learn from failures — and a number of approaches get a consistent thumbs-down.

Top of the list of less successful approaches is acquisitions and mergers. Numerous studies show that the odds of creating wealth via a major acquisition are low, in the order of one in four. The odds become even lower when the acquisition takes the company into new fields. Although 'sticking to your knitting' makes sense as a general rule, there are some spectacular successes in the 25 per cent of mergers and acquisitions that do create value for the acquirer. Examples include BHP, which progressed from selling steel to selling minerals and energy; Coca-Cola Amatil, which moved from tobacco to soft drinks; and GE, which shifted its focus from appliances and is now an industrial and financial conglomerate.

Another 'what not to do' is to become a fervent disciple of one of the quick-fix techniques, such as re-engineering or TQM (total quality management). But, again, these techniques became popular because they worked spectacularly well for some companies — not all companies. Motorola seemed to lift performance by focusing on very high quality standards — its so-called six sigma approach. Likewise, Toyota's lean production has now become the standard in the automobile industry and in many other areas of business.

Hiring a big-name chief executive from outside the company can also be risky. Jim Collins takes this line of thought even further in his book *Good to Great*. He asserts that 'celebrity leaders who ride in from outside are negatively correlated with taking a company from good to great'.[6] Ten of the eleven 'good to great' chief executives profiled in Collins's book came from inside the company. As always, there are exceptions to this rule too, such as Lou Gerstner at IBM and Bob Joss at Westpac.

The application dilemma

The four hallmarks of success—a strong strategic position, the right people, happy customers and financial discipline—are like Warren Buffett's investment criteria. They are helpful theories (and you ignore any of them at your peril), but they are also inadequate in several respects.

All the prescriptions for business success are imprecise and difficult to apply in the shades of grey that define the real world. That's why, rather than debate the nuances of competitive position in the market, Jack Welch came back to a simple rule: 'If you aren't in the top three get out'. It's also difficult to define what makes a person 'right', to balance the needs of different customers while delighting them all and to be financially disciplined without stifling innovation. What seems a prudent investment to one person may seem like a foolhardy risk to another—and theories don't help you decide where to draw the line.

Even if you want to apply the prescriptions, it is impossible to do everything at once. Fairfax faced challenges in every area: the strategic position was eroding, people management was poor, customer relations needed improvement and financial discipline was weak. Defining each challenge, deciding what to do and then coordinating action into a multiyear program is hard but important. Given the problems involved it is perhaps not surprising that this receives much less attention in the literature about sustained success than, say, the search for high profits.

No matter how self-evident the prescriptions for success may be, applying them on the job requires dealing with real people. Convincing people to understand, agree with and enthusiastically follow a strategic direction is at least as important as defining the direction in the first place. Rivalry, history, interpersonal relationships, ambition, biases, prior beliefs and lack of ability can derail the most elegant strategy. A good example at Fairfax was the launch of the ill-fated commuter paper, the *Express*, in Melbourne.

It was almost impossible for a serious broadsheet company to produce a tabloid with light news, strong entertainment and gossip designed to appeal to generation X and Y commuters who didn't read broadsheets. Fairfax people couldn't help producing a little Melbourne *Age* because of the traditions that defined Fairfax's journalism. The company was naïve to think that the tabloid publisher in Melbourne, News Ltd, wouldn't respond with a similar product that better reflected its tabloid history. Traditions can be changed, but they generally can't be changed quickly or easily.

As the studies show, for every rule or guideline there are exceptions — people who break the rules and yet produce dazzling results. I looked hard for acquisition opportunities, despite academic studies predicting a one-in-four likelihood of success. I believed the company could increase these odds by careful and disciplined analysis.

The challenges faced by companies seen as exemplars, such as GE, Westfield and Macquarie Bank, were quite different to those encountered by Fairfax and many other companies that aren't consistent winners. The books about excellent companies don't mention flawed strategies, high costs, a dysfunctional culture and structure and a lack of success. Most literature assumes that these fundamentals are in place and then focuses on what is special about the business. Yet I believe muddled companies like Fairfax are more common than excellent companies or consistent winners. Most managers face significant remedial work before they can single out one or two excellence attributes to focus on. Concentrating on islands of excellence before the basics are fixed is unlikely to work.

Although these four keys to success provided me with some valuable starting points, they did not provide a formula or roadmap that I could use with any degree of precision or confidence. I decided that I would have to work out a recovery strategy for Fairfax by myself.

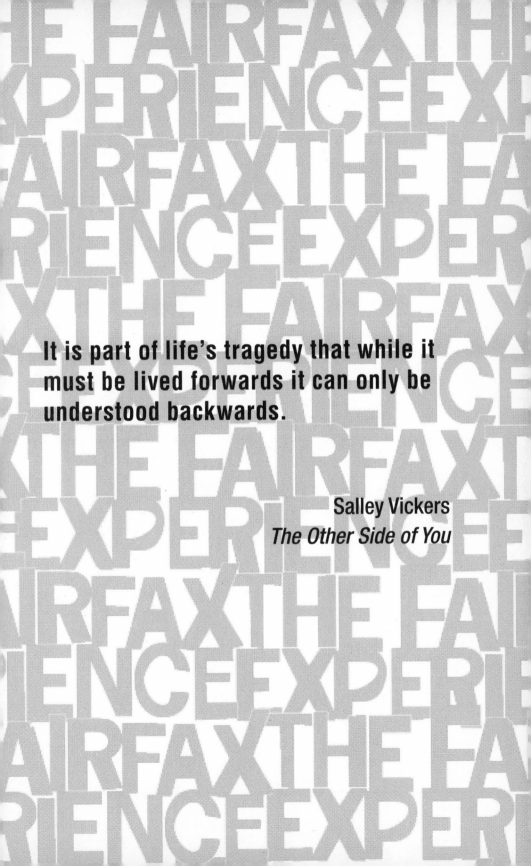

It is part of life's tragedy that while it must be lived forwards it can only be understood backwards.

Salley Vickers
The Other Side of You

Chapter 3

The Fairfax experience

Although in hindsight it is easy to describe the route I took at Fairfax, I didn't start at the company with a clearly defined strategy or a compass. I started with fires to fight and breakages to repair. In particular I had to cope with pressure from the board and the market to cut costs while also addressing my own concerns about the company's poor processes, infrastructure and strategic position. Fairfax first had to deal with the threats to the classified revenues of its metropolitan newspapers. Cutting costs, stemming the company's declining market share, and changing the structure, management processes, culture and infrastructure were all necessary to tackle this task, but I felt instinctively that the company needed to build up other areas of business that made sense to Fairfax in the long term. The internet, regional and community papers, magazines and Business Media were prime candidates for growth. However, the company also needed to look outside the square (even though the shareholders and board were not supportive of moving into new fields). Competition for buying media assets is intense, and I was not convinced that new, organically grown businesses would reduce the company's dependency on the metros from 74 per cent to my goal of 25 per cent in a five- to ten-year period.

Each of these two agendas—shoring up the metro business and building new businesses—posed quite different challenges. There was no quick-fix solution for the metros, which required major change in every area, including people, capability, processes and culture. The metros were facing attacks on many fronts, rather than a single threat that was amenable to a solitary, focused response, such as significantly improving journalism or building a new printing press.

Similarly, the second agenda, building new businesses, could not be carried out within a short time frame. It is almost impossible to buy businesses according to a deadline—I would have either paid too much or, worse, bought assets that turned out to be duds.

Clearly, I could not make, nor could the company absorb and implement, changes in all these areas at once. So the company ended up with a phased program that worked through each of the seven problem areas over a number of years. One of the things I am most pleased about is that the shape and direction of this program continued after I handed over the chief executive role to David Kirk.

Even after I spent seven years working on these issues, the task is ongoing. I often wondered how, with chief executive tenure now between four and five years, such fundamental changes in a large company can be properly handled by chief executives with much shorter tenure than my seven years. Even the legendary Jack Welch, credited with transforming GE, saw little progress during his first six years as chief executive and ended up staying in the job for twenty.

Counting the costs

The one problem area the company and its critics in the market did acknowledge and agree on was its high-cost structure. In the 1998 financial year reported costs grew by more than 8 per cent—not only was this well ahead of inflation but if left unchecked it would have sunk the ship. The board felt that it was under pressure from the market to act, so in the vacuum left by the resignation of chief executive Bob Muscat in August 1988, chair Brian Powers publicly committed the company to cutting $40 million, close to 5 per cent, from its cost base in twelve months. Due to this pledge my first year was preoccupied with cost reduction.

By the time I joined Fairfax in October 1998, the cost-cutting program, dubbed Project Hercules, was in full swing. Teams were at work across the group implementing the findings of a report prepared by management consultants McKinsey & Co. Although the cuts were to go deep, the plan was an uncontroversial mix of waste reduction, staff cuts and streamlined management processes. There were also some naïve suggestions, such as cutting the size of *Good Weekend* magazine from its elegant large format to the size of *Time* magazine to save on the cost of paper. *Good Weekend* is a unique size and advertisers are willing to pay a premium to appear in the format. Cutting the page size might have saved millions but only at the cost of even more millions in revenue!

Project Hercules

Although I was publicly committed to Project Hercules, it was very much designed to hit a one-off target rather than to contribute to the long-term capability building I felt the company needed. Brian Powers had announced the $40 million target because he was under pressure from the market to act. Normally this sort of announcement would be the job of the chief executive and I think it was a mistake to announce a target before a new chief executive was in place. Although the target was reasonable, if it had turned out otherwise another chief executive would have departed, causing even more instability. After all, Bob Muscat quit his post partly because he did not agree with the decision to hire management consultants or set cost-cutting targets.

Chair Brian Powers had chosen the figure of $40 million after being advised by McKinsey & Co. that it was achievable. However, there was nothing in the Hercules plan that clarified why costs were escalating, why Fairfax was a high-cost company and what skills and systems were needed in order to prevent costs rising again. In my view, dealing with the problem was like treating cancer — you can surgically remove the outward symptoms (costs) but if you fail to cure the underlying cancer the symptoms will just grow back.

It soon became apparent that Project Hercules was not going to deliver $40 million in the time frame the board and market expected. Some of the savings ideas that were supposed to follow from consolidating finance functions such as immediate staff reduction, or the introduction of a new editorial IT system and digital photography, would take a few years to implement. Other ideas, such as reducing the size of *Good Weekend* were plainly not cost effective.

In a tight situation my get-out-of-gaol card was purchasing. I found that little purchasing was done by competitive tender. Changing this turned out to be an immediate winner and a key factor in allowing me to tell the market that the company had cut $40 million in my first year. For example, contracts for telephone services were awarded to different providers across the business. Bundling Fairfax's phone services and putting the tender out to market produced enormous savings, not just in rates but also in administration. Newsprint was another area that saw significant cost savings. Instead of renegotiating the price every year on a three- to five-year contract, the company moved to a ten-year contract with a cap and collar (in the event that prices rose or fell outside agreed limits). These arrangements also saved time the company would otherwise have spent each year on negotiations. Over time every area was retendered and further savings continued to flow into areas as diverse as air freight, ink and spare parts.

Better ways of working

Rather than perpetual cost-cutting 'sheep dips', or short-term solutions, I regarded the search for better ways of working as the key to continuous improvement in costs. You can't cut costs effectively if you don't know precisely where the costs are — so I ensured the management team knew them inside out. If newsprint went over budget we had to have a proper discussion about why: was it because of production waste, because too much editorial was run or because too many copies were printed? Of course, if costs were high because more advertisements were being run then it wasn't a problem, because the high costs would be covered by more advertising revenue.

I regarded the search for better ways of working as the key to continuous improvement in costs

People and paper accounted for 64 per cent of costs in 1998 so each of these costs was tackled directly. Fairfax renegotiated the enterprise bargaining agreement that determined wages, reduced staff numbers via voluntary redundancies, spent capital on new plant that required fewer people to operate and renegotiated newsprint contracts. The company also introduced performance pay to reward managers for increasing circulation, meeting budget targets and achieving cost targets.

To develop managers' capabilities in business process improvement, I hired Professor Geoff Eagleson from the Australian Graduate School of Management to train about 400 people. The two-day workshops were not enough to fully develop managers' skills, but they did give people an understanding of business process, flow charting and how to identify sources of waste and errors.

The company then did some in-depth process engineering at *The Australian Financial Review*, which involved tracking the daily news flow from the morning editorial meeting through to publication. Fairfax found that stories were being filed by journalists right at the end of the day, that most were being touched up to thirty times by the writer, editors and subeditors and that a lot of this work was being done between 5.00 pm and 7.00 pm. It meant extra casual staff members were needed to cover the busy period when in fact most of the work could be done earlier in the day. Instead of just hiring more subeditors and leaving the *AFR* to operate as it always had, the paper redefined its process to do more work earlier in the day and to touch stories less. These actions underpinned excellent cost performance for a number of years.

For process engineering to work you need someone who is committed to realising its benefits. There was a committed editor at the *AFR* but it proved more difficult with editors at the *Herald* and *The Age*, where change was needed most. Because journalism remains largely a craft based on individual talents and initiatives, the idea of analysing and reorganising work flows is seen by journalists as 'management speak' and is actively resisted in newsrooms. Although journalism accounted for less than 25 per cent of total costs when I joined the company, there was still considerable room for process improvement.

The weight of symbolism

The cost-cutting exercise was also undermined by the company's anachronistic symbolism. Where Kerry Packer and Rupert Murdoch housed their media headquarters in modest offices, Fairfax had moved out of its shabby old premises to nine floors of prime office space overlooking Sydney's Darling Harbour. The company relocated in 1995 when it was rebuilding itself after receivership, and it reinforced the belief that Fairfax's problems were just a temporary glitch. Renegotiating the lease in 2002 led to a saving of around $1 million a year, but the symbolism survived. At the time of writing, my predecessor, David

Kirk, has announced that Fairfax will shift its Sydney headquarters to a more suitable high-tech site in Pyrmont, on the fringe of the CBD.

The belief that Fairfax's future would be a continuation of its glorious past was embedded in the building and reflected in everything the company did. For instance, I had a tough time arguing with management and senior staff that all employees should fly economy class on short-haul domestic flights. The management group thought this should apply to everyone except it and argued that at the very least I should fly business class. I held my ground on the decision, but even the airlines had trouble with it and consistently upgraded me to business class.

I did manage to close down the internally staffed commercial kitchen that could serve up to sixty meals in four dining rooms alongside the boardroom, choosing instead to outsource catering when required. And I did sell the outdated art collection that lined the walls on the executive floor, but it took four years. Instead of art that reflected what the company could once afford, the staff's photos, cartoons and illustrations were displayed to showcase what the company did and had reason to be proud of. I bore a lot of criticism for selling the collection but, in hindsight, I should have sold it earlier. The auction of the art collection by Sotheby's in November 2002 grossed $2.4 million in a sale that *AFR* writer Terry Ingram wrote 'did not sparkle because of a lack of fashionable modernists'.

....

Mrs Simpson [descendant of Fairfax founder John Fairfax] thought the auction was 'scandalous. It's such a shock I'm speechless.'... John B. Fairfax said yesterday: 'My view is that there is no better place to house them than in the corridors of the company that acquired them.'

Valerie Lawson, *The Sydney Morning Herald*, 26 September 2002

....

A shrinking market

Cost management was important but it was no defence against the threats to Fairfax's market share. The *Herald* and *The Age* were at the core of the company's business and formed the basis of its identity, but the global market for classified advertising in newspapers was in steady decline. Classified advertising revenues were under threat from the internet, electronic media and specialist publications. Yet Fairfax remained oblivious to the extent of the challenge due to its poor market intelligence; when it did respond it was with a bandaid—raising advertising rates and cover prices.

Fairfax remained oblivious to the extent of the challenge due to its poor market intelligence

My starting point for understanding Fairfax's market challenge was a broader comparison of the competition along the lines of the 'share of stomach' approach used successfully at Coca-Cola Amatil (see chapter 2 for more on this strategy). So when measuring its share of job advertisements Fairfax began including internet job sites, radio, television and specialist publications with job listings for comparison. The process was complex and took a number of years to complete. Part of the problem was finding a measure that would enable the company to compare Fairfax's print employment ads with those in other media, such as the internet and radio. The only meaningful comparison was dollars spent, but this data was not readily available and could only be estimated.

Selling the company short

Better market intelligence was accompanied by improvements in selling. The advertising sales team operated on the assumption that Fairfax was such a pre-eminent media institution that active selling was unnecessary. A senior sales executive summed up this attitude when he told me his job was akin to standing in a wind tunnel with his coat open, catching orders as they blew in. The marketplace was a little less sanguine. I asked some of the country's top ad buyers, including the legendary Harold Mitchell of Mitchell and Partners, to rate the company. The results were damning. I was told Fairfax had lovely salespeople who were pleasant to deal with, but who left money on the table and were rated below average in terms of their effectiveness in solving client problems.

Part of the problem was that the *Herald* and *The Age* acted like silos with no cooperation or coordination. If Mercedes-Benz wanted a page-three advertisement in both papers a single salesperson could not deliver this result. The two papers even negotiated discounts on a different basis. For major corporate deals across all Fairfax papers and websites, anywhere from five to nine people would front the client! Fairfax had the same ad buyers back two years later, after implementing a number of changes, including centralising some responsibilities, and introducing training and performance management. They found that Fairfax's salespeople were up to the industry average and improving, which I felt was great progress.

Change was a little easier at Fairfax's major contact centres, or phone rooms, where operators took calls from prospective advertisers, mainly for ads in the classifieds. When I started, the contact centres were professionally run but essentially intended for taking orders. Later on, when Fairfax was doing due diligence at the *Trading Post*, I discovered that the *Trading Post*'s contact centres were completely different. Its operators were looking at the ads in Fairfax publications and calling advertisers to persuade them to try the *Trading Post*. They were actively selling as well as order taking and they were being paid incentives to do so. Some of the regional and community contact centres, such as at the *Newcastle Herald*, were also proficient at outbound selling. I was able to introduce similar techniques at Fairfax's major contact centres and build a motivated sales force that was prepared to make things happen. The wedding page of Sydney Sunday paper *The Sun-Herald* presented a good example of active selling. By using the phone directory and calling potential advertisers, Fairfax's operators put together a directory of wedding suppliers opposite the 'wedding of the week' photo spread. These and other similar initiatives stemmed the bleeding in classified revenue significantly.

The products of trial and error

To expand into new markets and reduce reliance on the *Herald* and *The Age*, Fairfax needed to develop new products, but the early initiatives all failed. At a disadvantage because of my lack of industry experience and history, I badly underestimated the depth of rivalry and animosity between Fairfax and Rupert Murdoch's News Ltd.

Fairfax launched *Express*, a daily commuter tabloid, in Melbourne amid much fanfare. The concept had been tried successfully in London, and Fairfax thought that if it could be first to launch a similar Australian product that it too would experience such success. But the move was trumped by News Ltd, which copied the move and secured a contract to hand its commuter paper, *MX*, out at railway stations. In hindsight, Fairfax should have known that the staff of *The Age*, a quality broadsheet, could never hope to beat News Ltd at its own game and produce a racy tabloid for an audience of young city commuters. News Ltd also had more to lose if *Express* was successful, because a new tabloid competed more directly with its *Herald Sun* than *The Age*.

In addition, News Ltd matched Fairfax's launch of *The Central Coast Herald*, a daily, paid newspaper designed to service the rapidly growing commuter area north of Sydney. News Ltd responded by flooding the market with its free local paper, which it quickly began publishing almost daily. Fairfax produced a quality paper with dedicated journalists and community support, but it eventually had to admit defeat and fold the paper back into its sister publication, the *Newcastle Herald*. Although defeat was bruising, it was a Pyrrhic victory for News Ltd. Fairfax probably lost about $1 million on the exercise, but losses were contained because the company piggybacked the launch off the *Newcastle Herald*. By comparison, it was estimated that News Ltd threw close to $10 million into the fight. It not only published more often, but it also handed out its paper at railway stations, ran huge advertisements and slashed advertising rates.

My first acquisition, a small business-magazine publisher called Strategic Publishing, also took many years to turn around. The purchase price was a modest $20 million, but it took an enormous amount of work to meld the entrepreneurial, shoot-from-the-hip culture at Strategic with Fairfax's business. The two mistakes made by the company were to not install its own chief financial officer from day one and to not have sufficiently detailed acquisition and post-acquisition plans.

Fairfax also spent years looking at buying the local arm of Canada-based *Trading Post*, but the business was eventually sold to Telstra for $635 million — well above Fairfax's offer in a complex auction process. I copped a lot of flak for 'losing' the *Trading Post*, but in the end you have to know your price and live with it.

After these false starts Fairfax began to hit its straps by focusing more closely on its sustainable competitive edge. The clear competitive strength of the *Herald* and *The Age* is the quality of the readership in terms of income and education. Alan Revell, publisher of the *Herald* and *The Sun-Herald* at the time, came up with the idea of *the(sydney)magazine*, a super, high-quality glossy published monthly and inserted in the *Herald*. The quality of the audience and the product allowed Fairfax to reach new advertisers rather than cannibalise existing ones. Revell was so confident about the concept he bet his bonus that he would make budget. Advertisers loved the product and, even better, News Ltd couldn't copy it. News tried a lesser quality magazine in *The Daily Telegraph*, but it was a financial disaster because the company was printing about 400 000 copies to Fairfax's 150 000, and it couldn't deliver the wealthy audience needed to make the numbers work. Excluding launch costs, *the(sydney)magazine* was profitable from its first issue. The concept was later introduced successfully to *The Age* in the form of *theage(melbourne)magazine*.

Next Fairfax launched zoned real estate classified sections in the *Herald* to target its wealthy readership in the north, east and inner west of Sydney. Local community newspapers were attacking the *Herald*'s real estate classified market with attractive glossy products. But once Fairfax's new printing plant was up and running it was able to print high-quality colour advertisements at low cost and insert these in zoned editions of 'Domain', its existing midweek homes section. Domain was also the name of the company's real estate website—and the cost to list on it was included in the sales package to agents. This package was also something News Ltd and competing suburban papers couldn't replicate, and it was profitable from its first year.

A structural shift

The organisational structure I inherited in 1998 was the corporate equivalent of a large but dysfunctional extended family. The publishers of the major mastheads openly competed and refused to cooperate with their sister publications. Advertising sales were completely decentralised, major and minor mastheads reported directly to me and the internet was lumped in with overall corporate strategy (for more information on Fairfax's organisational structure in 1998, see appendix E). The structure made it impossible to manage and control costs and resulted in a poor focus on profit and loss. The structure might have been great for independent journalism, but in my view it had the potential to destroy the company.

The organisational structure I inherited in 1998 was the corporate equivalent of a large but dysfunctional extended family

In early 1999, soon after taking over, I tried to tidy the mess and reduce the number of people reporting directly to me from eighteen to twelve (for details of Fairfax's revised organisation structure in 1999, see appendix F). I created a group operations division and hired Peter Graham, who had been chief executive of Pacific Power during my time as chair, to run it. This brought publishing services, printing, pre-press, national distribution, IT, purchasing, transport and facilities management under central management, providing significant cost savings and administrative advantages. It took eighteen months to pull together but was well worth the effort.

At the same time, I streamlined the publisher structure. *The Australian Financial Review* and business magazines were brought together to form Fairfax Business Media. I also formed a magazines cross-masthead group and put the internet into a separate operating division called f2. In addition, regional newspapers were taken on by Alan Revell, publisher of *The Sun-Herald*. The main publishing silos at the *Herald* and *The Age* remained intact.

In the early days I tried to keep the existing senior staff in place and promote talent from within the organisation, but few of the publishers had the necessary business skills. I also found it difficult to keep an ongoing dialogue with *The Age* in Melbourne during these crucial early years. So in 2002 I streamlined the structure again. I swapped around the publishers of *The Age* and the *Herald*, moved *The Sun-Herald* into the newly named Herald group and created a commercial division under Nigel Dews comprising the internet and metropolitan print classifieds.

However, the issue of cooperation in editorial display advertising between *The Age* and *The Sydney Morning Herald* remained, so a year later I made the controversial decision to adopt a functional structure for the metros (to see the organisational structure of Fairfax in 2003 to 2004, turn to appendix G). Instead of a publisher in each city, I had an editor-in-chief at both papers reporting to a central editor-in-chief. Likewise, I ensured that advertising and marketing in both papers was controlled by a single commercial director. I realised this was not optimal and that it might result in losing local focus, but I saw it as the only way to significantly improve journalism, advertising sales, marketing and cost control at the two papers while also enabling new printing capacity.

Mark Scott was appointed editor-in-chief of the *Herald*, *The Sun-Herald* and *The Age*, while Alan Revell was appointed commercial director. Major gains in efficiency were made, and the structure also helped in the start-up phase of the new printing plants in Melbourne. However, it was an imperfect arrangement, so in 2005 I reverted to installing local managers accountable for profit and loss at each paper, albeit suited to managing directors with a business focus, rather than publishers with editor-in-chief roles.

After the New Zealand acquisition of INL, Fairfax considered a number of structural options that would serve the growing organisation. The structure I left for my successor in 2005 had seven people reporting to the chief executive (see appendix H for Fairfax's organisational structure when I left).

After seven years of evolution, seven of the original eighteen executive team remained, five in new roles and two, Michael Gill and Gail Hambly, in similar roles.

The search for a successor

By late 2003 the board was actively searching for a new chief executive. My contract was for five years and I had to make a decision about whether to continue after my five years were up in November 2003. I was prepared to stay but didn't want another five-year contract. I'm a fix-it-and-build-it person who enjoys a strategic challenge and I realised I could take on one more challenge provided I left Fairfax before I was much past sixty. In the end I agreed with the board to continue until the end of 2005 or until a replacement was found.

Finding a successor was not easy, so I was required to stay until November 2005. Brian Evans, who ran the regional newspapers and then the New Zealand papers so successfully, was one possibility, but in the board's view he lacked the financial and strategic experience necessary to run Fairfax. My preferred candidate was David Kirk, but he had just taken on the top job at PMP, Australia's largest printing business, and didn't believe it was proper to move. Meanwhile the board was pursuing Douglas Flynn, head of UK media buying giant Aegis, but it was unable to reach terms. The board was running out of options and I was keen to commence the next phase of my life. I went back to David Kirk, who I knew would have fulfilled his initial commitment at PMP by mid 2005, and invited him to lunch. We ate at a club that was well out of the public eye and shared a bottle of wine, which was unusual for both of us and an indication that we were ready to do business. David agreed to be a candidate and meet with the chair and then the board selection committee; he became the next chief executive of Fairfax. Brian Evans ended up leaving to assume David's old job at PMP.

Management processes and information

On a recent business trip to Singapore I asked a Singaporean colleague how long I should schedule for an important meeting with a senior government official. He observed that meetings where things get done take fifteen minutes whereas meetings where nothing gets done take forever. I have an extremely low tolerance for meetings for this reason, but I believe they are a necessary evil.

When I arrived at Fairfax there was no regular cycle of meetings because there had been no long-serving chief executive to establish a pattern—which is possibly why few people understood what was required of them. Staff members would turn up with mountains of data and slides and read every page to me. Their intentions may have been good, but they were undermined by an infuriating assumption that I couldn't read! I encouraged people to deliver more concise reports, but they were still not in place when I left seven years later.

A system of regular weekly and monthly meetings evolved. There was a weekly meeting (or 'weekly beating', as mentioned earlier) held one-on-one with my executive team. These meetings were designed to enable me to keep in touch with all areas of the business. There was also a weekly numbers meeting with my top team, called the EMT (executive management team), to review weekly performance reports for each part of the business.

In addition, I held monthly meetings with the senior managers and editor at each business unit (for example, the whole team at the *Herald*, *The Age* or *The Australian Financial Review*). Even more important were monthly strategy discussions involving all my direct reports, which were held off-site, away from the distractions of the office. The rule on these occasions was that we discuss strategy, not operational matters. The aim was to create new options for the business and enrich the ideas list.

One of these off-site meetings gave me a great insight into how the media industry works. I had suggested a few early rounds of golf before a 9.00 am working session in the club house. I chose a golf club in Sydney where Fairfax had a corporate membership. What I didn't expect was a News Ltd photographer with a long lens. The next morning we were pilloried over two pages of *The Daily Telegraph*, whose writers asked what sort of company allowed its leadership to swan around playing golf. The irony was that in my time Fairfax was the frugal mouse of the Australian media industry when compared with the lavish junkets, such as overseas trips and luxury boating, enjoyed by those at Murdoch's News Ltd and at the Packers' Publishing and Broadcasting Ltd.

....

In times of crisis, true leaders dig deep and pull something out of the bag. But if you're a top-level Fairfax executive, the only thing being pulled out is a five-iron. With the circulation of the company's newspapers plummeting and staff morale lower than a Tiger Woods scorecard, Fairfax CEO Professor Fred Hilmer this week summoned his inner circle troops for a two-day 'crisis' conference at the very plush and very exclusive Terrey Hills Golf and Country Club.

Peter Holder and Jo Casamento, *The Daily Telegraph*, 24 January 2001

....

Although I had mixed success with golf, the retreats provided useful insights into the business and how key players viewed its future. One of Fairfax's more successful retreats was held at Sydney's Olympic stadium about the time of the 2000 Olympic Games. Close to one hundred people attended the event to talk about the business plan and outlook. On this occasion I used ex-teacher and sports coach Tony Goldsby-Smith as a moderator. He used a simple framework to look at where the company was, where the leadership team would like it to be and how to get there. After listening to team discussions Tony asked how many people thought the company was moving purposefully into the future; he received an overwhelmingly negative response. Essentially, people were saying that the company had no growth and was drifting. Despite the negativity, it was a really valuable insight that triggered significant action and an example of the positive role a good moderator can play. (I discuss the importance of dealing positively with negative factors in chapter 6.)

The final piece of the puzzle was the quarterly forecast meeting. These were tough for all concerned because it was there that it was decided whether to upgrade, downgrade or stay with the earnings expectations that were in the market. Although I was keen to keep the team focused on the big picture, I also knew the market would punish Fairfax for any short-term fall in earnings or any downgrade.

These meetings were supplemented by the annual budgeting process and a three-to-five-year strategic planning cycle. These plans were typical of what other companies did, but the rigour and realism that underpinned them needed improvement.

A culture adrift

Culture was by far the toughest nut to crack at Fairfax. This was partly due to the traditional, craft-based origins of the company, but it also had a lot to do with a high turnover of chief executives, which had left the organisation rudderless.

In sailing, the default position is into the wind—meaning that if you take your hand off the tiller of a yacht it turns into the wind and the boat stops. At Fairfax I found a culture with a number of default positions—and they all headed into the wind, halting Fairfax's progress.

So if you took your hand off the tiller of costs, they went up, never down. The direction I wanted to shift the tiller to was a position where people thought about costs as if they actually owned their part of the business.

Similarly, if you took your hand off the tiller of investments people would always opt for the best and most expensive option. Even when this was changed by centralising control of capital, the reputation for big spending stuck!

I am still accused of 'gold-plating' the printing plant the company built from scratch at Tullamarine, west of Melbourne. During the surface excavation some huge boulders were uncovered that normally would have been hauled away at great cost. Instead, the decision was made to stand them upright, sprinkle gravel around them and make a striking stone garden reminiscent of Stonehenge, and that never needs watering. Many questioned these actions, dismissing the garden as a waste of money. They assumed that because the building was Fairfax-owned, that the rocks would probably be imported.

In fact, the Tullamarine plant was built for roughly 15 per cent less per unit of capacity than the last printing plant built in Australia. Although it was a low-cost construction it took a major effort to complete the operation. Tough industrial disputes in which Fairfax stood its ground against building and print unions ate into the schedule and challenged Fairfax's default position, which was to compromise.

Editorially, the company's default position was to turn left and be agenda driven. I tried to ensure coverage was balanced, although I did not interfere in editorial unless errors of fact or serious bias were brought to my attention. Editorial decision making tended to be based on issues, rather than analytical thinking. This meant journalists often conducted campaigns where they persisted in covering stories long after readers had lost interest. Lack of cooperation between mastheads was also a drag on progress.

The first big sign that the silos were being broken down was the 2001 story exposing rape allegations against the then head of the Australian Torres Strait and Islander Commission, Geoff Clark. The story was broken by *The Age* and shared with the *Herald*, but there was and probably still is underlying resistance to the concept of copy sharing.

I was trying to foster a meritocracy with pay based on individual as well as team performance

In terms of people, the default position for Fairfax was egalitarianism, whereas I was trying to foster a meritocracy with pay based on individual as well as team performance. In a traditionally heavily unionised area such as journalism this takes time. It was not until the second three-year industrial agreement with journalists that I was able to embed the notion that senior people in particular had to earn their pay rises, rather than having their salaries indexed automatically for inflation.

Fairfax was in the unusual position of having two sets of customers—readers and advertisers—with competing interests. The default position on the readers was that they were lucky to have Fairfax, whereas I wanted them to feel valued and listened to. Advertisers were treated with distrust, especially among editorial staff, whereas I wanted them to be treated as partners, within certain limits. The tension this causes is evident when newspapers consider putting advertisements on the front page. Readers expect the front page to be the most important news. Advertisers would prefer more of it — or even all of it — to be used for advertisements. Similar conflicts of interest arise with the front pages of sections. I believed the front page of Fairfax's papers should be restricted to news; I was prepared to stick with this even when important advertisers, such as Toyota, were keen to buy the whole front page and the competition was happy to oblige them. But I was willing to have advertising on the front pages of sections such as real estate. Fairfax had an industrial dispute over this issue with journalists in Melbourne, but I refused to budge and after a day they backed down.

In terms of the market, Fairfax's default position was to be a victim. The company was always the one that was going to be taken over or have business stolen from under its nose. Instead, I wanted to foster a proactive culture in which Fairfax was the aggressor. In fact, the company bought a lot of businesses and sold very few. It bought the New Zealand papers, Text Publishing, RSVP, Strategic Publishing, the *Port Stephens Examiner* and other community papers. (Soon after I left, the company also bought the New Zealand-based online auction business Trade Me and then the *Border Mail*, an important regional paper.) Fairfax sold Australian Geographic because it was basically a retailer and sold its stake in telco AAPT because it didn't fit Fairfax's business, but that was about it. It was a case of the myth defying reality — and the myth was that Fairfax was a poor little company, even though its market capitalisation almost doubled to $4 billion in seven years.

Changing an entrenched culture is not easy. I spoke a lot about being competitive and proactive, and put out a values statement that reinforced this, but it was of limited use in a cynical organisation suspicious of management speak. I believe the only way to deal with such trenchant opposition is to walk the talk and let the facts speak for themselves. At Fairfax that meant the company would make acquisitions, be polite to readers, work better with advertisers, reward merit and reject business cases that were not supported by analysis. There were discussions about editorial, balanced reporting, turning down over-inflated investments and continuing to keep a close eye on costs. Culture changes when you do things differently but it takes time. After so many chief executives some of the old hands probably thought my days in the top job would be numbered and they could wait me out. It didn't work for them this time.

Printing plants and brick bats

One of the things that shocked me most after joining Fairfax was the amount of money needed to replace outmoded or poorly chosen physical infrastructure. But spending was crucial for making cost savings elsewhere and providing the capacity to grow the business. It took five years and more than $300 million to get a new printing plant up and running in Melbourne and to refurbish the Sydney plant. It cost another $100 million to replace a galaxy of IT systems that were outmoded and unable to talk to each other. Similar but smaller projects were undertaken in pre-press and distribution, but the most public and expensive initiative was undoubtedly the printing plants.

Melbourne had a printing plant that was unable to meet on-time running, the colour needs or capacity requirements of *The Age*. At best it could only print 25 per cent of the paper in full colour. Some Saturdays *The Age* came out so late people joked that it was an afternoon paper. The presses were housed below the editorial floors in a Dickensian building in Flinders Street. The site also had a history of poor industrial relations between staff and management.

Building the new printing plant at Tullamarine alongside a major freeway was one of my first decisions, and it provided a real plus for distribution. It involved not only transferring staff, but also reducing staff numbers from 280 to 160. The then secretary of the Australian Manufacturing Workers' Union, Craig Johnston, identified the move and loss of jobs as a rallying point. One Wednesday afternoon the union issued an ultimatum stating that all existing staff members should move to the new site on their existing conditions of employment or the paper would not be out on time. When management resisted, staff walked off the job and blockaded the printing press. Despite a number of executives losing a night's sleep trying to find a way to get the paper out, for the first time in its history, Fairfax lost an edition of the *The Age*. If you are never prepared to accept a loss due to industrial action the union has you over a barrel, so it was a worthwhile battle to fight. The board was supportive and the reaction from advertisers was positive too. The sun rose as usual the next morning and staff began discussions with management.

Peter Graham tried meeting with Johnston privately but Johnston did not seem interested in constructive negotiation. The installation phase at Tullamarine was delayed by three months to sit the union out on the issue of staff selection. The union wanted to retain staff based on seniority whereas Fairfax wanted to select people based on merit. There was further industrial disruption after the move to Tullamarine, but the plant eventually came in under budget at $220 million.

After the dispute was resolved I held a lunch for the management group who built and commissioned the Tullamarine plant. I presented each member with golf balls inscribed with the names of the union heavies who had made the job of building and staffing the plant so difficult. On golf courses around Sydney and Melbourne mysterious golf balls with union leaders' names printed on them are still turning up.

At the same time, Fairfax undertook a $90 million upgrade of its Chullora printing plant in Sydney. It was first completed in the 1996 financial year, but the demand for products had changed and the plant could no longer handle the number of sections and full-colour pages that were required. Both plants were up and running in 2004.

Unlike the experience at Tullamarine, there were few industrial problems at Chullora, possibly because the battle had been won when the plant was first constructed. In fact, when I made visits to Chullora most of the questions raised by the printers were about the Fairfax share price. It was almost like a shareholders' meeting, with questions about the classifieds market and the profitability of the Saturday papers. The highest take-up of the employee share-ownership scheme was at Chullora, where most people took their full $3000 entitlement. Many had been given shares at $1 in the float, which quickly went to $3, so they had had a good experience of the sharemarket and took an active interest in their investment.

There was tremendous interest in the construction program from industry analysts, although a lot of it was mischievous. The company's biannual briefings always saw groundless rumours aired. Two favourites were that the roof at Tullamarine leaked and that it was not high enough. Then there was the story that Fairfax didn't need the plant any more because the paper was getting smaller, and the company was therefore building capacity for demand that would never eventuate. The assumption, fuelled by critics at rival publications, was that Fairfax was incapable of best practice in any area of the business and was building capacity unnecessarily. Murdoch's journalists were happy to write that until News Ltd announced it was spending $500 million on new printing capacity in Australia. The real value of Fairfax's new presses was the ability to print full colour, which enabled its publications to carry far more attractive sections and different sorts of advertising.

Interestingly, over the years, Peter Graham and I made several approaches to News Ltd about sharing plant and offering each other backup in case of power failures or other disruptions. We believed it was in neither party's interests for one company to have a paper run late, because newsagents would invariably wait for the late paper before starting their deliveries. I had a very cordial meeting with Lachlan Murdoch and he agreed that cooperation made sound financial sense, but we underestimated the fierce historic rivalry between the two groups. Peter Graham had more luck with his counterpart, George Calvi, head of operations, and on one occasion Fairfax helped out News Ltd with spare parts after it had a plant failure. However, I believe management at News Ltd put a stop to any further outbreaks of goodwill.

Setting a strategic course

Fairfax owned two great newspapers in the *Herald* and *The Age* that were at once the company's greatest strength and its Achilles heel. The core newspaper business was being threatened on all sides by intense competition from other print media, radio, television and the internet. These alternative sources of information were competing for Fairfax's most precious commodity—readers—and its primary source of revenue—advertisers. As I've mentioned, years of instability in ownership and leadership had left Fairfax directionless at a time when it needed to focus on its future survival.

In many ways Fairfax faced challenges similar to those experienced by all mature, single-product companies. So I set about implementing a classic strategy tailored to the Fairfax situation—consolidation of those areas where it had a competitive advantage and the taking of calculated risks on new areas of activity. The aim was to scale back Fairfax's reliance on the metros by altering the business mix.

I chose to consolidate the metros' position through strategic acquisitions in adjacent areas of the market, notably suburban and regional newspapers. These are unglamorous businesses but potentially highly profitable, especially when they can be worked alongside the metropolitan papers to produce economies of scale.

Targeting familiar businesses also allowed Fairfax to use its market intelligence to buy companies that were underperforming or undervalued by their present owners.

Consolidation coupled with acquisitions is a difficult double act in any company, and it was particularly hard for me to explain and carry out given that I was a newcomer to the media industry. Neither the board nor the staff was comfortable with the premise that the two pillars of the business, the *Herald* and *The Age*, had a limited future. In addition, neither I nor my management team had the skills in buying media assets that the old hands, such as the Murdochs, Packers, Stokes and Rural Press Ltd, did.

My natural inclination for developing strategies in this situation was to move via what the US management scholar Brian Quinn calls 'logical incrementalism'. I knew broadly what I wanted to achieve and sought to create and grab opportunities that would take Fairfax in that direction, subjecting each one to careful logical analysis. But I had no master plan for designated takeover targets and deadlines.

My early efforts were not encouraging. As already discussed, the acquisition of Strategic Publishing in Singapore took considerable effort to avoid loss of value. The launches of *Express* and *The Central Coast Herald* failed. Agreement on an acceptable price for the *Trading Post* was never realised, and online acquisitions, such as CitySearch, became casualties of the dotcom bust in early 2000. Meanwhile, the company's shareholders were lobbying the board for bigger dividends and no further acquisitions.

It was against this background that in 2003 Fairfax reached agreement with News Ltd and other shareholders to buy INL, the major New Zealand publisher in which News Ltd held a controlling interest. At the time I was subjected to a barrage of negative press from competitors. The Packers' *Bulletin* devoted a major story to my 'disastrous purchase' under the title 'The fall of Fairfax'. I was told the champagne corks were popping at News Ltd!

Fred Hilmer says the INL deal shores up the future of Fairfax. But many others say it looks more like a tombstone.

John Lyons, *The Bulletin*, 26 August 2003

For News to sell newspapers is a very rare occurrence. Perhaps the best analogy is a case of 'the fish John West rejects'.

Mark Westfield, *The Australian*, 16 April 2003

Reports of the death of Fairfax were greatly exaggerated. New Zealand–based INL delivered a stable of local and national newspapers and magazines, including *The Dominion Post* in Wellington, *The Press* in Christchurch and nationals *The Sunday Star Times* and *Sunday News*. The group was peripheral to News Ltd's business, and I believed News Ltd needed to sell assets to cover its DirectTV purchase. A good price was offered and News Ltd agreed, but it then turned around and said it had sold Fairfax a dog. Fairfax's shares were marked down as a result, but the war of words spurred its and INL's management to work extremely hard proving News Ltd wrong.

The [INL] acquisition was one of the greatest successes during my tenure

Profits from New Zealand were up about 60 per cent in the first two years under Fairfax's management, and profit margins before interest and tax were close to 35 per cent. This was possibly due in part to a strong New Zealand economy, but also because the assets, being peripheral to News Ltd, were under-managed when Fairfax bought them, as the company's due diligence suggested. The acquisition was one of the greatest successes during my tenure and probably added $1 billion to the value of Fairfax over and above the purchase price.

Fairfax's other major diversification was the internet, where it spent close to $150 million on start-ups and acquisitions net of asset sales. The company had been reasonably successful at implementing websites for its publications and classifieds, but it did not have the top sites in key areas, such as employment and real estate. In these areas start-up companies founded and run by entrepreneurs were beating traditional media companies to the punch.

Fairfax built an auction site but sold it for a significant profit after concluding that it could not compete with eBay. The company went into and out of shopping. It also bought the local licence for the US-based CitySearch online directory, which came with a second telephone directory called Big Colour Pages. It turned out to be a major diversion for the company and only ever lost money. The institutional shareholders hated it and wanted Fairfax to close it and walk away. In the end the phone directory business was closed, and CitySearch was sold to Telstra for about $20 million, which took some of the pain out of the mistake. I personally thought the company should have persevered with CitySearch, but the board didn't have the stomach for it and the market would have hammered the venture.

In 2005, after Fairfax had consolidated its position, the company started hunting for acquisitions again and bought the dating site RSVP, which turned out to be a fantastic purchase. Dating was a traditional classified category that used to be in newspapers and here was an opportunity to claw some of that business back. RSVP was the leading dating site and would have been costly for competitors to attack. The business was purchased for about $40 million and according to analysts at the time it could have been sold a year later for many times that price.

There was also a view to floating off Fairfax's internet division, as the Packers had done with NineMSN, and the company had a number of banks working on the proposal. One of the Packers' strengths was the way they acted like a mini merchant bank focused on strategy. They did some great deals with Microsoft, eBay and Seek, the leading Australian employment website. They also beat Fairfax to a car sales site it should have bought. However, the Packers had their own difficulties in the new space, such as the spectacular One-Tel collapse and their selling out of eBay. Critics were saying I should raise new capital for Fairfax's digital expansion — as the Packers were doing — rather than rely on old company dollars. But the Packers' site was not in direct competition with their old media interests, as Fairfax's would have been. It would have created difficulties having one set of shareholders with internet rights to the *Herald* and another set of shareholders with print rights. If another entity owned the internet business it would not necessarily work cooperatively with Fairfax's publications.

A recent UBS report forecast earnings before interest and tax of $42.2 million for Fairfax Digital in 2006–07, excluding any contribution from New Zealand online auction site Trade Me, which was bought after I left. That is a 28 per cent return on a business on which Fairfax spent $150 million to $200 million building from scratch, net of asset sales. Adding Trade Me would boost estimated 2006–07 earnings to $76.8 million, or 14 per cent of Fairfax's total earnings.

The final score

By sticking to its strategy Fairfax managed to reduce its dependence on the metros from 74 per cent of the business mix in 1998 to 46 per cent in 2005. Although Fairfax had lost some circulation share in the metros due to tight controls over marketing costs and distribution, circulation numbers were improving by the time I handed over. Group revenues grew from $1.1 billion to $1.8 billion thanks largely to the New Zealand acquisition and greater contributions from regional and community newspapers and Fairfax Digital. By 2005 the New Zealand operations accounted for 28 per cent of revenue and about one-third of profits.

New Zealand also accounted for most of the $1.67 increase in the Fairfax share price from $2.87 to $4.54 during my seven years at the helm. The company paid about $1.1 billion for INL and it is probably worth over $2 billion today, which translates into a gain of about $1 a share. Of the remaining $0.67 cent increase, more than $0.20 came from organic growth in Fairfax Digital and the remainder from tightening costs.

Table 3.1 (below) shows that group earnings more than doubled in seven years from $112 million to $253 million, lifting earnings per share from 13.9¢ a share to 25¢. Shareholders also received growth in dividend income from 9.5¢ a share to 23¢. To put this in perspective, total shareholder returns at Fairfax over the seven years were about 9 per cent a year, the average for the company's international peers. Of ten major newspaper organisations with similar portfolios only Johnston Press in the UK and The Washington Post Company performed better (see appendix B for a comparison of the annualised total returns of international newspapers in this period).

Table 3.1: key changes at Fairfax

	1997–1998	2004–2005
Earnings	$112m	$253m
EPS	13.9¢	25.5¢
Share price (October)	$2.87	$4.54
Dividends	9.5¢	23.5¢
Underlying cost growth	8%	2%

The changing business mix and improvements in earnings and revenue growth were achieved by working on the seven problem areas identified at the outset. Although the company made significant inroads in all areas, there was considerable unfinished business. Between 1998 and 2005, growth in costs was reduced from more than 8 per cent a year to 2 per cent; however, the metros' cost structure is still too high to justify complacency.

Fairfax went some way towards addressing its eroding market share through improvements in measurement, client-focused selling, product initiatives and strategic acquisitions. But these advances were tenuous in a market experiencing long-term decline. More organic growth in the digital area and more initiatives like *the(sydney)magazine* and the localisation of Domain are needed to maintain a competitive edge. And the challenge of finding and then making value-adding acquisitions remains.

The organisational structure I left for my successor was streamlined, functional and far more effective than the one I inherited. Internal promotions were more likely than they had been, and some of my people were being hired to good jobs elsewhere, a sure sign that Fairfax was growing its talent. Editor-in-chief of the Heralds, Mark Scott, has been appointed the managing director of the Australian Broadcasting Corporation; Alan Revell, who was a key player in some of Fairfax's best product initiatives and acquisitions, was hired by the Daily Mail Company's internet business in the UK; and Fairfax New Zealand chief executive Brian Evans is now chief executive at printing group PMP.

Although many individuals within the organisation developed their talents and careers, the corporate culture was far more intransigent. It is difficult to change a culture developed over more than a century in a highly visible industry like newspapers in the space of a few years. But it must change if the company is to flourish. Improving physical infrastructure was easy by comparison. The company now has the printing plants and IT systems it needs to work effectively and grow.

Lastly, but most importantly, the company now has an identifiable and appropriate strategy to take it forward. There is still much unfinished business but it is in a far better position to build on its strengths and shore up its weaknesses. By the time I left, Fairfax was a good company, not a great one—but I regarded 'good' as a solid achievement.

It is not the critic who counts, not the man who points out how the strong man stumbles, or where the doer of deeds could have done them better. The credit belongs to the man who is actually in the arena, whose face is marred by dust and sweat and blood … if he fails, at least he fails while daring greatly. So that his place shall never be with those cold and timid souls who know neither victory nor defeat.

Theodore Roosevelt
'Man in the Arena' speech
23 April 1910

Chapter 4

In the hot seat: the decision environment

Being catapulted out of an advisory and research role into an active position in a troubled company brought home to me the chasm between theory and practice in a way that no amount of studying could. I'm not one to denigrate theory (as Karl Weick wrote, nothing is as practical as a good theory), but in the people-dominated, political and competitive world of running a large enterprise good theories are at best a starting point for real-world action. Even with good theories, such as those on competitive advantage, you have to be able to make them work.

That is why people who teach general management and strategy often do so via an analysis of real business cases rather than lecturing on theory. Because the cases are based on real-life situations they give participants a chance to see how complex it is to develop a strategy or to apply even a simple idea, such as achieving a low cost position or improving customer service. I used cases almost exclusively when teaching strategy and employee relations courses at the Australian Graduate School of Management; but the method has its limitations.

The discrepancies between carefully selected case studies and the real world became stark once I took on the chief executive role. On reflection, four differences stand out for the chief executive: time pressure is constant and acute; most information is incomplete and may be inaccurate in important respects; judgements, particularly about people, are critical; and all the players have considerable emotional capital at stake when making critical decisions.

To put it another way, in practice decisions are made on the hop and based on incomplete information, gut feel and emotion, as well as logic. As a result, our aspirations, biases, attitudes and judgements about people shape our decisions as much as facts and logical analysis. In this chapter I describe the environment in which I operated and made decisions.

The ticking clock

When I worked as a consultant and academic there was plenty of time for writing, discussion and analysis. At university I could schedule classes and meetings in the afternoon so that I had the mornings to myself to turn the phone off and research or write books and articles. At McKinsey & Co. my fellow consultants and I had three-month units of work, which allowed us to follow an idea through, test it, kick the tyres and see if the idea held up to scrutiny. By contrast, as chief executive of Fairfax I had very little unstructured time. To me it was a big culture shock not to have time to follow things through or ponder what will work. You are expected to hire other people, such as McKinsey & Co. consultants, to do that. A chief executive never has time to form perfect, logical solutions to problems that arise almost daily.

To illustrate the busyness of a chief executive's day I have pulled out two days from my diary during my time at Fairfax and included them in appendix I. The first entry is a relatively normal day and the second includes investor presentations, which were a major part of my job. Every day was like being in a dentist's surgery — calling 'Next! Next!', seemingly always running late and having a constant flow of people through the room. Phone calls and emails also took up a large part of the day, but they were not scheduled so could be wedged in between meetings or handled while in the car.

In a normal week there was a mix of internal and external commitments. Internally I would have a group meeting with everyone who reported directly to me as well as a weekly one-on-one with each of them. Something I learned from Fairfax chair and US investment banker Brian Powers was that given the importance of short-term operating issues at Fairfax, it was good practice to schedule an hour with everyone once a week. This allowed time to go over the live agenda, beginning with strategic matters and then moving on to operational matters. So, for example, when *The Australian Financial Review* was moving to introduce a new desktop product, AFR Access, it was top of my list of priorities when I spoke with Michael Gill, head of Fairfax Business Media. I felt a lot of the company's projects did not have enough input from readers and other users so I wanted to stay in touch with the endeavour. Even with inevitable missed meetings due to travel and other business demands, with anywhere between ten and twelve people reporting to me these weekly one-on-ones easily consumed a full day a week.

On top of these meetings with the management team there were monthly (later bimonthly) board meetings and regular and irregular board committee meetings. With so much time spent in meetings it would have been easy to never leave the office. So in order to stay in touch with the business I tried to schedule walks around editorial, the printing plants and other parts of the business. I also tried to make time for informal chats with staff when needed, either with groups or sometimes with individuals (for example, when someone was at a point of making a career decision and his or her manager had suggested the staff member talk with me).

Then there were the infamous Saturday morning phone calls about late newspapers, which also ate into my time. I thought it crucial that the paper reached readers on time on Saturday because if you can deliver the big Saturday edition on time you should be able to do it every day. Although being an hour late is not good practice it generated few complaints on Saturdays, when people rise later than on weekdays. However, if delays went beyond an hour I had to be phoned with an explanation and the action taken. These calls played havoc with my golf game on far too many occasions. The people at the plant knew they could catch me in the car on my way to golf around 7.00 am. After a bad call it would take me four holes to settle down.

These meetings with my peers were useful at a time when media reform was on the national political agenda

The demands on my time from outside the company were just as pressing. I talked to other chief executives in the industry, both locally and overseas—and every time I did it in public it was a news story. If I bumped into James Packer and chatted there would be reports that Publishing and Broadcasting Ltd was buying Fairfax. So meetings were clandestine. I always met Kerry Stokes, owner of the Seven Network, for coffee at his home on the way to work. Nick Falloon, the head of the Ten Network, and I used to meet at the American Club, and if I met with the Packers it would be at their Park Street, Sydney headquarters. Again, when discussing options for Rural Press Ltd I met Brian Macarthy at a small North Shore restaurant not chic enough to be frequented by high-profile media people. Likewise, when Ian Law, the head of West Australian Newspapers, and I were discussing a possible merger we met with our chief financial officers in an Adelaide hotel room, halfway between our Sydney and Perth bases.

These meetings with my peers were useful at a time when media reform was on the national political agenda. There were other issues discussed too, such as press freedom and anti-terrorism bills that contained some draconian measures, and my peers and I had some good wins. My meetings with politicians were always time consuming because they insisted on spending time on Fairfax's coverage of them or their party. I was encouraged by the fact that politicians of all persuasions complained equally loudly, so the company's coverage must have been unbiased!

I had most to do with News Ltd when Fairfax was buying its stake in New Zealand newspaper group INL, and News Ltd was probably the hardest to deal with. Soon after I joined Fairfax, News Ltd invited me to visit its London plant as an example of what could be achieved. I saw this as a positive step. As discussed earlier, the company also tried a number of cooperative ventures, but it was difficult to make the relationship work because News Ltd executives were obsessed with Fairfax's editorial coverage of the Murdoch family. Fairfax papers broke the story about Rupert Murdoch and his third wife, Wendi Deng, having a baby and ran a lot of commentary about the effect it might have on the family's succession and inheritance arrangements. The Murdochs themselves were incensed. I think they thought I should approve and edit every story about them, or at a minimum 'deal with' the editor and journalists whose work had offended the family. My view was that my role was about the integrity of the reporting—not the colour of the reporting.

Big advertising customers would also occasionally give me a roasting over Fairfax's coverage of their company or products. One such case involved a review of a new BMW in 'Drive', the *Herald/Age* motoring section. BMW was promoting the car as extremely high tech and intuitive to drive, so the paper got three highly intelligent people to test-drive it. Everyone had difficulty using the technology—even starting the car was counterintuitive. So a subsequent story ran with a digitally altered image of the BMW image melting down the page. It would be an understatement to say that relationships with BMW, a key advertiser, were strained. However, if Fairfax was to repeat advertisers' claims without question, the paper would soon lose its franchise with readers and then advertisers wouldn't want to advertise with the company anyway. This leads me to another time pressure: the need to meet advertising customers and media buyers at social events like the Melbourne Cup, so that they felt they could comfortably pick up the phone and talk to me. Although I was prepared to listen sympathetically, I made it clear that I did not write the paper and would only intervene in cases of inaccuracy or serious bias.

Then there were board meetings at Westfield Group, where I was deputy chair. I drew criticism from the Australian Shareholders' Association as well as from the Westfield Group and Fairfax shareholders for serving on the Westfield board. The issue for all three was not about conflict of interest but about the time I was spending away from Fairfax. In their view, a chief executive should spend 100 per cent of his or her time in the company. Westfield was not a big advertiser, and even though there were times when Fairfax publications ran stories critical of the company I never received a phone call about any of them from the Westfield executive chair, Frank Lowy. I assume this is because Lowy is on the board of the Daily Mail Company and understands how the media operates. Being on the Westfield board gave me a window into one of the best-performing companies in the world. I often came back to Fairfax with good ideas about the way Westfield Group planned, managed its staff and handled the new corporate governance agenda.

Incomplete and misleading information

If textbooks underestimated the time pressures faced by chief executives, they completely understated the problem of incomplete and misleading information. Delving into the Fairfax accounting system was like stepping through the looking glass and into Wonderland.

Accounts may be soporific but poor accounting makes it extremely difficult to make good decisions. As a consultant you take sound accounting practices for granted, but in practice I found myself grappling with the details of management accounting to understand short-term performance and emerging trends. Provisions are a good example. Each division needed to provide funds in its accounts for factors such as staff leave or bad debts. Establishing the provision or setting aside funds showed up as an increased cost; when the provision was reversed, such as when leave was taken or the bad debt collected, reported costs went down. I felt that sometimes these provisions were being used to smooth costs between good and bad months. A certain amount of smoothing is fine, but the way it was practised at Fairfax lacked transparency. Because Fairfax was run as a series of fiefdoms, and every paper was doing its own provisioning, I did not know the true weekly operating performance; for example, were costs high because a provision had been made for leave or because staff had been added? I dealt with accounting problems by centralising accounts under the chief financial officer, Mark Bayliss.

Allocations were another problem area. One seasoned accountant at Fairfax told me that Fairfax accounting was all about doing business with itself. There were multiple transactions between mastheads and divisions and every time a transaction took place there was a cost, making accounting very expensive. Worse still, people would often explain away a poor result by saying, 'It's not me, it's allocations'.

Circulation estimates were also inaccurate. I wanted to receive circulation estimates every week, taking into account adjustments for waste, returns and trade copies. The first few estimates in a six-monthy audit period tended to be positive until about a month before audits—then the estimates would change for the worse. This was not evil behaviour, just human nature. Some staff members would stick with their positive estimates despite evidence to the contrary, hoping that something good would happen. Sometimes managers would say they had a special promotion coming up that would boost circulation, therefore supporting the estimate, but when pressed for details they would simply promise to come up with something.

Management control is about understanding why things are not as you were lead to expect. In order to have an intelligent discussion about costs you need to know why costs are incurred. But unless you do proper variance analysis of the difference between what is and what could be, all you get is stories that are an extrapolation of one day's experience generalised over a month. Take staff costs: if they are higher than last year that can only be because you hired more staff or you are paying existing staff more. Additional staff could be casual or permanent. Higher pay could be attributable to overtime and allowances, a higher base rate or some special deal. Unless you understand what drives costs you can't deal with the problem sensibly. This sort of analysis did not happen at Fairfax until some years after I took over. As a result, management spent too much time guessing and having unproductive discussions.

Management control is about understanding why things are not as you were lead to expect

By comparison, information about tactical moves in the industry was quite accessible because the media is such a 'leaky' industry. (For example, if you are going to launch a new product you won't be able to keep it secret because you will have to tell your advertisers to draw their support.) But in a more fundamental way Fairfax had poor market intelligence because it was operating in an industry where market strategy often remained in the heads of media proprietors.

Information from outsiders could also be misleading. Government intentions were difficult to determine because ministers tend to tell you what they think you want to hear. I lost count of the number of times media legislation was about to be enacted during my seven years in the job, and I spent a lot of time working on the issue.

It can also be difficult to find clear legal advice. When retrenching staff I wanted to be a good employer and follow best practice, but I also needed to meet the requirements and interests of shareholders. This required predictions of the way industrial tribunals might rule, which could be difficult. In practice, tribunals seemed to rule in favour of employees, more, at least, than I was advised was likely to be the case.

When bad news is buried

There are two parts to the problem of incomplete and inaccurate information. The first is that you are flying blind, and hence you will inevitably make costly mistakes. The second is more subtle: when information is incomplete or wrong, that part often turns out to be bad news.

Most accounting, circulation or marketing 'surprises' were bad. Whether it is a general human tendency or not—I believe it is and discuss this in chapter 5—certainly at Fairfax there was a strong culture of not being open about problems for fear that it would be construed as weakness. The best example of this was at *The Age* when the company was building the new printing plant. At the time, *The Age* felt pressure on margins from high costs and its declining advertising markets. Pressure from the advertising markets was hidden by raising prices, and high costs were hidden by cutting costs in the advertising department while holding editorial costs steady. The hope was that management could keep milking advertising to support editorial—but it was not sustainable. Redundancies followed and Fairfax had to rebuild the advertising areas that had suffered. I could see what had been going on when I pulled it all apart, but it took a while for me to see the pattern. There is a strong forensic side to being a chief executive that can be very time consuming when people are obfuscating.

The attitude towards information and its quality affects all aspects of decision making within an organisation. It has an impact on where you focus attention and what targets or benchmarks should be set. Fairfax was less transparent than other organisations I have been exposed to, due in part to the turmoil caused by the revolving door at the top. A sense had developed that the chief executive would not get involved in operational detail because he or she would not be there long enough. In fairness to previous chief executives though, if you walk into a company with ownership instability and liquidity issues then you have to deal with those first. After all, if you can't pay your bills everything else is secondary.

The quality of information also affects personnel because it allows you to assess who is doing a good job and who isn't. Judging personnel is particularly hard for an outsider. Rupert Murdoch, Frank Lowy and Kerry Packer could rely on superb networks of people they appointed and had known for decades. Their information flow would be far more balanced, reliable and complete than mine would have been as a relative newcomer. I found that this information problem did diminish considerably after a few years; but even with better information, chief executives are often working with less information and less accurate information than would be desirable. So judgement and intuition become all important.

The role of judgement

The dual pressures of time and incomplete or misleading information mean the role of judgement is critical. The chief executive must make intuitive judgements about people's veracity and reliability as well as about markets and opportunities. This is especially difficult when the chief executive is appointed from outside the company and the industry.

People

Looking back, I believe there are three types of behaviour that I need to recognise and take into account when assessing the reliability of what I am being told: optimism, a tendency to generalise and passion.

Optimism is generally reflected in the omission of bad news rather than the commission of deliberate deception. One example at

Fairfax was the loss of part of the Victorian State Government classified advertising business from *The Age* to rival Melbourne paper the *Herald Sun*. I only heard the government was thinking about removing the ads once the situation had reached crisis point and the business had been put to tender. If I had been alerted to the problem earlier I could have spent time with the client, discovering why it was unhappy and trying to sort things out. Once the situation was at tendering stage it was too late, and the *Herald Sun* underbid Fairfax. Another example occurred when a big advertisement placement company was unhappy with the way it was being treated. I didn't hear about that from my advertising people but from the chief financial officer. Because I had proper notice of the problem, I could ensure the company's concerns were addressed. These are just two examples of people concealing a problem they were not dealing with effectively.

The people I had the biggest problems with were the seasoned Fairfax hands, rather than the people I appointed. When you arrive at a company with a confronting agenda—namely, that the company's two iconic newspapers are not going to be central to its future—it is hard to deliver the message without demoralising staff. If you are a journalist or an advertising sales executive then hearing that message is not going to help you do your job, it is going to make you want to leave. So people tend not to hear the message and bury any news that reinforces this negative view of the business.

The second type of behaviour I identified was the tendency of some managers to generalise. When classified advertising declined, as it did periodically because of the influence of economic cycles, some were quick to tell me 'it's structural'—meaning other media, such as the internet, were getting the business. The implication is that there is not much you can do. Another generalisation put to me, for example, was that circulation was under pressure because the retail newsagency system was deteriorating. In each case, much more is going on than a structural shift or a change in the fortune of a type of retail outlet. I came to hate generalisations, such as 'we are transforming our relationships with customers', 'we are fundamentally changing how we manage our people' or 'we are putting an innovative structure in place'. These statements mostly turn out to be empty words. The people involved had not carefully dissected their problem, so I couldn't rely on improvements being made.

The third type of warning–light behaviour is passion. People with a passion for their work, the product and the customer are precious, and turning down their ideas and potentially demotivating them is hard. However, there is a dark side to passion, particularly in a creative business like media. Passion blinds people to the reality that their idea is not viable.

People like Alan Revell, who came up with the concept of the successful *the(sydney)magazine*, and Michael Robinson, who devised Domain Local, were passionate about what they were doing, but they also knew their customers and costs intimately and achieved results. But there were also plenty of people who were equally as passionate about things that didn't work. The digital team was highly motivated but many of its ideas were flops. Luckily, the team was in a growth area so the occasional failure did not deter it. Failures are a necessary part of coming up with new ventures, but they must be outweighed by success.

Generating profitable growth opportunities in news was much more difficult. People were passionate about expanding Fairfax's coverage of the arts in the 'Spectrum' section on Saturdays, for example, but the initiative never produced the higher advertising revenue they hoped and believed it would. The revamped Spectrum created a better Saturday package but it did not alter the fundamental economics of the paper. Despite a number of major redesigns at the *Herald* and *The Age* and the introduction of new sections, there was no increase in circulation that could be linked to an editorial initiative. Higher circulation was only ever driven by things such as sales and discounting, putting papers in petrol stations and promotional activity. I eventually became cynical and told people that they had to give me an advertising case for any new initiative no matter how passionate they were about it or they would not get the money. If people said it would raise the profile of the paper I would ask them to show me one reader who would buy the paper that otherwise would not. I also insisted that advertising sign off on any changes because editorial was often keen to leave advertising out of the loop. In the end you have to make a judgement not just about people's passion but also about their ability to deliver.

The market

The other big judgement call is about the market you operate in and, in the case of a media company like Fairfax, whether current conditions are cyclical or the result of a more fundamental structural problem. This issue permeated Fairfax's decisions, as cyclical change requires quite different action to structural change. If a downturn is cyclical, you tighten your belt and wait it out but keep developing the business. If a downturn is structural, bigger challenges, such as searching for new business opportunities, must be faced.

You have to make a judgement not just about people's passion but also about their ability to deliver

The purchase by Fairfax of the INL newspaper business in New Zealand was another case of judgement about a market and a buying opportunity. Critics of the purchase said Fairfax had been lucky that the market had gone its way, but luck had little to do with it because the company had done extensive preparatory investigation. Fairfax looked at the company as well as the market it operated in and did not just rely on Reserve Bank of New Zealand figures. Brian Evans, who was to become chief executive of New Zealand operations, rode around Wellington in taxis getting a feel for the city and asking contacts in local companies about the advertising environment. At the same time, James Hooke, Fairfax head of strategy, carried out detailed due diligence. People joked at the time that Fairfax bought in New Zealand because it was my favourite walking holiday. In fact, because I had spent so much time in and around Queenstown on New Zealand's South Island, I could see the tourism and development boom had not reached its peak.

Judgements about people are something you can't learn from a book. Instead, you learn from experience with people who deliver on what they say. It is easy to make a prediction about someone you have worked with for many years, but difficult with people you have just met. People may be charming and persuasive (after all, they want to be liked), but data may be hidden and a positive spin put on stories. Clearly, judgement is critical for managers and it only improves with time.

Nobel laureate and authority on human decision making Herbert Simon demonstrated the importance of expertise and experience in decision making in his classic study of chess masters. He randomly assembled chess pieces on a board and then asked chess masters and amateur players to replicate it from memory. Both rookies and masters completed the task with about the same degree of accuracy. Then he arranged the chess pieces in formations you might expect to find in a real chess game. The masters replicated the board perfectly, but the rookies failed. Simon described expertise as a memory bank of up to 50 000 situations that could be applied to current problems. The theory is that once people master an area it enables them to learn and recognise patterns that have occurred in their area of expertise and link them with potential results.

Simon's findings explain why I could readily make judgements about strategy and processes in people-intensive businesses (because I had been doing it for thirty years) but could not as easily make judgements about ad markets and printing technology (because I didn't have the depth of expertise that comes with time). In his book *Good to Great* Jim Collins argues that chief executives from outside the business or industry are generally not as successful as internal candidates.[7] Although I would have been more successful at Fairfax if I had had more direct experience of the company and the media industry, candidates with media industry experience lacked expertise in strategy and business processes. Given that the board had to make a trade-off between the two, and in light of the types of problems I found, I believe the board did the right thing, whether it chose me or someone with a similar background.

Emotional capital

Up to this point I have argued that optimal decision making is impaired by a lack of time and information, forcing the chief executive to fall back on judgement. There is, however, an added complexity: judgements involve significant emotional capital and ego. I once interviewed a PhD student who wanted to test the theory that success for chief executives is inversely proportional to the publicity they receive — that is, the more a chief executive's ego is on the line the less able he or she is to make good judgements. A recent study of German football referees found that referees were statistically biased in favour of the home team not because they were affiliated with the home team but because of the mood of the crowd watching them. Could it be that the decisions of business executives are similarly compromised by fear for their reputation and the roar of the crowd? I don't know if the PhD student's theory was ever tested but my time at Fairfax convinced me it was worthy of study! As chief executive of a large media organisation I found myself in a goldfish-bowl and under public scrutiny in a way that I could not have imagined.

I had previously enjoyed a good relationship with the press during my time as an academic, management consultant, director on public company boards and chair of the National Competition Policy report for the Australian Government. In these roles I generally assumed the expert role for the business press. As chief executive, however, I was not an expert but, rather, a personality. When I had lunch with someone from the media industry it would appear the next day in the business gossip columns. Likewise, when my wife and I sold our house it rated a story in *The Daily Telegraph*. I tried to keep my family out of the limelight, but my wife, Claire, was caught out once when our younger daughter married and wanted a wedding photo to appear in Fairfax's Sunday paper, *The Sun-Herald*. A gossip columnist from the daily sister publication, the *Herald*, received wind of this and rang Claire. Claire said she didn't seek publicity and didn't want to talk about it. A caustic piece then appeared quoting Mrs Hilmer as saying she was not interested in publicity but that the wedding would be fully covered in the *Sun-Herald*! Ultimately, when you are a media figure everything you do classifies as news—which is how I justified Fairfax's coverage of James Packer's private life when he complained (he was unmoved).

> **Ultimately, when you are a media figure everything you do classifies as news**

Extensive coverage is not restricted to media industry players. Anecdotally, it appears the personality cult around chief executives is more intense in Australia than elsewhere. When Bob Joss came from the US to lead Westpac Banking Corporation he commented that the media coverage he experienced was far more intense than he had been used to back home. He was suddenly a personality.

Media interest properly extends well beyond the gossip columns. For a company like Fairfax, business decisions, results, investor reactions and competitive tussles are all conducted in public, with liberal quantities of comment and opinion to complement the facts.

The media scrutiny intensifies the emotional capital tied up in business judgements and decisions. If you make an earnings prediction then you are held to it, which puts a lot of emotional pressure on you. Once earnings guidance was given to the market, the top team felt enormous pressure to deliver. Some might argue that this is a good incentive to perform, but it is only a few steps away from doing 'what we can' to doing 'whatever it takes'—and the incentive is entirely short term.

No matter what you do, most reporting is negative. At one point I had an analysis done of Fairfax, News Ltd and Publishing and Broadcasting Ltd coverage. Each story was classified as positive, negative or neutral. Over the years, I received a barrage of complaints from both the Packer and Murdoch families about Fairfax's coverage of their private lives and business succession issues; yet Fairfax was no more negative in its coverage than they were. The default position of all three media companies reporting on the media industry was negative. Tellingly, although News Ltd was slightly less negative about itself than its competitors, the company was not even consistently positive about itself.

It is emotionally difficult for people to receive constant negative feedback. It tends to make managers averse to risk, less open and reluctant to confront mistakes, take a write-off or remove something or someone that is not working. Competitors face the same emotional challenges and this colours the way they deal with you. In Australia the media is a largely dysfunctional industry because of the ego issues that spring from coverage; for example, newspapers were seriously under threat but Australia's print media players could not establish an effective industry bureau to promote newspapers. You couldn't get everyone in the room without bitter discussion about the latest piece of media coverage of one by another—although it's not surprising given the family dynasties that still dominate the Australian media scene.

As I discovered, studying managers and actually walking in their shoes are different propositions. Unlike an experiment in a lab, where you work in private and are judged by results, chief executives are carrying out the experiment while everyone is watching and judging before the results are in. When people are under scrutiny their ego becomes involved, and ego distorts perception and judgement.

If there is a positive in all this negative scrutiny it is that it ensures managers try extraordinarily hard to make things work. To make things work in an environment where decisions are bounded by time pressures, poor information, subjectivity and emotion, managers must interpret what they see and act accordingly—but chief executives too are human and subject to human biases.

A blind algorithmic approach usually trumps human judgement in making predictions and diagnoses ... human beings are inconsistent: we are easily influenced by the order in which we see things, recent experience, distractions and the way information is framed. Human beings are not good at considering multiple factors.

Atul Gawande
Complications

Chapter 5

The positive bias

I had only been at Fairfax a matter of days before I had to approve a proposal to sell Australian Geographic. Australian Geographic produced a fine magazine that was clearly compatible with Fairfax's core business, but it also operated retail stores selling products with a nature theme. Price and terms had been agreed with the prospective purchaser of the business. All I had to do as chief executive was sign the documents and collect the money. To my rational self this was an easy decision: Fairfax was not a retailer, retail was the largest part of the Australian Geographic business, the price was fair and I needed to strengthen the company's balance sheet ahead of upcoming expenditure on printing plant upgrades. Yet despite this logic I felt uncomfortable about selling assets and shrinking the company. I asked whether there was a way to at least keep the magazine business, but the two businesses were intertwined so it was all or nothing. Logic prevailed and in hindsight the decision was correct.

A few years later I faced a different kind of decision. Would Fairfax launch a new free commuter paper? The decision to launch *Express* was not easy, and it had an emotional side to it that was quite different to what I felt selling Australian Geographic. The business case was marginal; Fairfax would have to achieve economies of scale by covering both Melbourne and Sydney within one to two years with a largely common product. There were significant skill and logistics issues, but the project team excelled, finding ways to overcome obstacles. Eventually, the board, management and I decided to go ahead. I recall driving home just before the launch, reflecting on what we were doing, how this project had energised so many people and being pleased that after more than a year of cost reduction and downsizing the company was moving forward. Unlike my experience with Australian Geographic, my feelings about *Express* were all good, but ultimately the decision was bad.

On reflection these experiences highlighted the different emotional aspects of a positive decision, such as launching a new product, and a negative decision, including selling a part of the business. But there is a more general and important point to be made: there are emotional and perceptual biases in decision making that lead us to treat positive and negative decisions differently, for the most part overemphasising positives and underemphasising negatives.

Selling a business is harder than buying one so purchasers tend to overpay for acquisitions; on the other hand, sellers, being naturally reluctant, are the winners. Research consistently backs up this point. In day-to-day management, hiring, promoting, praising and rewarding are emotionally easier than firing, demoting, moving a person sideways, and reprimanding or penalising a poor performer. I recall how I felt before talking to an executive I needed to remove. No matter how compelling the logic, I felt bad and had to fight the tendency to drag my feet and avoid the meeting.

I wondered whether this was just me or whether other chief executives shared my dilemma. In conversation after conversation my peers told me their biggest regret was delaying difficult decisions about people. Eventually I realised I was not alone in my bias towards positive actions and experiences.

This bias is also evident in the weight of writing on management. The bestsellers are about growth, excellence, motivation, hoopla, celebration, incentives and rewards. The titles tell the story: *In Search of Excellence*, *Good to Great*, *Built to Last*. Similarly, most business biographies are about the pioneers, builders and developers: Jack Welch, GE; Frank Lowy, Westfield Group; Roberto Goizueta, Coca-Cola Amatil; and Sam Walton, Waltons.

The tao of management physics

As Newton discovered, for every action there is an equal and opposite reaction. The management parallel may be that in every positive situation there is an actual or potential negative. Unless a manager clearly sees and deals with both the positive and the negative aspects he or she is doing an incomplete job and performance will suffer. So a leading market position will attract fierce competition, product improvements that create a superior product may lead to complacency and a once highly effective manager with a top reputation may run out of steam. The bias in each case is towards not seeing the negatives — namely a threat, a product becoming obsolete or a good friend or old hand not performing. Conversely, the positives — a strong market position, a good

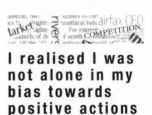

I realised I was not alone in my bias towards positive actions and experiences

product or a strong performer — tend to be seen through rose-coloured glasses. Yet even a good product may have flaws, and a strong performer may be unsuited to his or her changing role.

Consider the following examples of superior products: the Apple Mac, Sony's Betamax and Macquarie Bank's infrastructure funds. Market acceptance for each product was good and market leadership should have followed, but in each case there was a negative — a chink in the armour — for no product or service is ever perfect. The more successful something is, the more competitors seek to exploit its weakness. So IBM took on the Apple Mac with the PC, which set the industry standard and brought a host of new entrants into the industry. Likewise, VHS beat Sony's Betamax through better partnerships and distribution. Macquarie Bank's success attracted competitors, causing the value of infrastructure assets to rise and market superiority in time to become untenable.

Similarly, Fairfax had a leadership position in the metropolitan newspaper market in terms of market share and margins, but its so-called rivers of gold — the revenue it earned from classifieds — was a magnet for competitors. Although Fairfax was aware of the problem it was so fixated by its long-running rivalry with News Ltd that it underestimated the threats from suburban and specialist publications and the internet.

Another positive is innovation. Yet no sooner does one innovate when the potential for decay — the negative — emerges. Even Microsoft, one of the greatest success stories of the last twenty years, faces this problem. Microsoft, with its product range, distribution and relationships, dominates the PC operating system market. However, its price structure and sales approach opens the door for competitors such as Linux and Firefox, and its success attracts the attention of competition regulators. So seeing and then dealing with these negatives becomes as important for Microsoft management as developing the next generation of Windows.

The challenge of seeing and dealing with negatives, as well as positives, permeated my time at Fairfax; for example, the company's newspapers were continuously reinvigorated with a series of innovations. If you were to compare an issue of today's Saturday *Age* with an edition from ten years ago it would be barely recognisable due to its cleaner layout and its use of photographs and colour. The same is true for the *Herald* and *The Australian Financial Review*. Yet lurking behind these innovations was decay. As soon as a product was improved competitors would introduce better pictures, more appealing features or clearer indexing. In order to combat this Fairfax needed to make continuous improvements, but the pride that people rightly feel when they accomplish such improvements can quickly lead to inertia and complacency. Similarly, although praise for a job well done is important, nobody's performance, including my own, is completely praiseworthy. The negatives of honest performance appraisal, reprimands and even warnings or dismissals are as real and as important as the positives of praise, reward and promotion. Yet most managers dislike reprimanding a member of staff for making mistakes when on balance he or she has been doing a good job.

The idea as a matrix

The bias against negatives and towards positive experiences can be put into matrix form, a common management tool for summarising an idea and explaining how it might be applied. Figure 5.1 interprets the positive bias using a matrix model. The vertical axis deals with seeing and the horizontal axis is related to acting.

Figure 5.1: the positive bias in matrix form

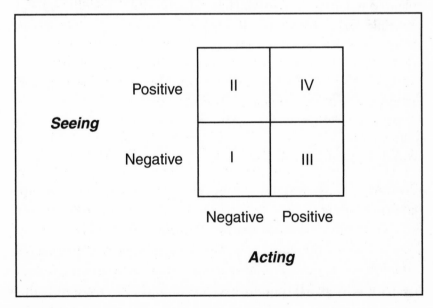

The quadrants are numbered from what I view as the hardest situation to identify and act upon (quadrant I) to the easiest situation to see and act upon (quadrant IV).

Quadrant I applies in situations where a manager needs to perceive a negative situation or problem and then take a negative action. (For example, a long-serving executive may not be performing well, leaving no alternative but to terminate his or her employment.) At Fairfax seeing a negative entailed accepting the decline in classified revenue at the *Herald* and *The Age* as inexorable; the negative action required was to continuously improve efficiency and reduce the number of full-time journalists. These types of situations pose the biggest challenge to managers because of the significant barriers to both seeing the negatives and taking negative actions.

In quadrant II the situation is perceived as positive but the action needed is negative. An example of this is an internet business growing but the team that started it needing to be replaced because it is not the best suited to developing the business's full potential. Another example may be that of a person doing a good job in a role that is about to be axed. These situations are also difficult, but generally less so than cases in quadrant I, because the positives in the situation are readily perceived.

Even easier to handle are situations that are viewed as negative — for example, high costs or poor service — but for which there is a positive course of action that will solve the problem (quadrant III). This may include investment in new technology or redesign of workflow coupled with retraining.

Quadrant IV covers the easiest type of situations: seeing an opportunity and going after it with money, people and time. For instance, at Fairfax it was recognised that the INL newspaper group in New Zealand presented an opportunity to buy an undermanaged asset. A team of people were assembled to assess the business over many months, and INL ultimately made an excellent investment.

For a company to continue to improve there needs to be a recognition that some things could be done better. In every leadership situation, whether it is a project, product or personnel decision, managers are faced with positive and negative elements of their decision.

Tough decisions remain at Fairfax

As I found tackling the negatives to be the toughest part of being a chief executive, it's not surprising that much of the unfinished business at Fairfax at the end of my seven years was in the negative areas.

Take Fairfax's biggest strategic challenge—the vulnerability of its metropolitan newspapers and the fragmentation of its audience as readers tuned in to radio, television, community newspapers, the internet and iPods. The positive response to the challenge was to acquire new businesses, enter into joint ventures, reinvigorate the existing business with new products and sections and put content onto new platforms. (For example, Fairfax did deals with Optus and Telstra to carry news on their mobile phones and introduced magazines and product improvements to carry more targeted display advertising.) The negative side to those initiatives was that they did not generate enough revenue to offset the drift of advertisers from Fairfax's classifieds. The company also needed to scale back, cut costs and restructure. Redundancies were inevitable and difficult. To go even further and suggest selling the *Herald* or *The Age*—potentially a sound strategy—would have been considered heresy.

Reducing the cost structure was also a top priority at Fairfax. On the positive side the company invested in plant and IT systems that allowed significant increases in productivity. (Fairfax, for example, replaced thirty people doing payroll on about ten payroll systems with a centralised system that required only ten or so people.) Replacing and upgrading printing plants allowed Fairfax to reduce the total number of printers by one quarter.) Although there were industrial problems at the Tullamarine printing plant, there was a general acceptance that if you spend a vast amount of money on new plant you need greater productivity from the staff that remains.

However, the negatives of cost cutting, such as retrenchments and continuous cutbacks, are not embraced with the same enthusiasm as positive actions.

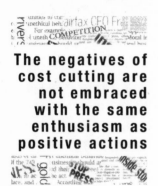

The negatives of cost cutting are not embraced with the same enthusiasm as positive actions

Lack of management depth and an intractable organisational culture were more difficult challenges. The positive action taken was to hire some talented managers from outside the business and to develop promising candidates from within Fairfax. But this could only be done with clear performance feedback, which many managers found difficult, especially in an organisation unused to performance reviews. In my first performance discussion with Robert Whitehead, who held a series of management and editorial positions, he told me it was the first appraisal he'd had in twenty years!

The positive side of culture was easy—namely, celebrating the best newspaper traditions. There were many ground-breaking stories over the years, notably reporter Paul McGeough's award-winning coverage of Iraq; the Bulldogs Rugby League Club salary cap scandal; the secret Swiss bank account dealings of disgraced stockbroker Rene Rivkin; and allegations of rape against Geoff Clark, then chair of the Aboriginal and Torres Strait Islander Commission.

There were also many occasions to celebrate getting the paper out against the odds. Newspapers thrive on crisis and handle these situations heroically. After the September 11 bombings, for example, the following morning's papers had to be completely redone around midnight. Yet there are times when you need to ditch traditions and recognise the negatives inherent in newspaper culture. With some exceptions for major news events, it's better to get the paper out on time than hold it up for late breaking news. Readers want to wake up to their newspaper on the lawn or they will stop buying it.

The positive bias of newspaper culture is to say yes, we can handle that fantastic late-breaking story and get the paper out on time, rather than recognising the negative and admitting that there is a high probability that the paper will be late.

Sources of bias

The environment in which a chief executive operates—the media, powerful advisers and service providers, suppliers of equipment and technology, and politicians—makes it easy to overemphasise the positives.

Chief executives operate in a goldfish-bowl and get their best media coverage for positive actions, such as buying companies, developing new products, technological innovation and hiring people. Executives such as GE's Jack Welch and News Ltd's Rupert Murdoch are lionised for their high-growth strategies. This is despite News Ltd not having been an outstanding investment over the last several years and Jack Welch's termination arrangements having been severely criticised. People will forgive you almost anything if you are growing.

Conversely, executives who are seen to be capable of handling negative actions tend to generate negative publicity and derogatory nicknames, such as 'Chainsaw' Al Dunlap or Max 'The Axe' Moore-Wilton. Al Dunlap earned his reputation for firing thousands and closing plants and factories at Scott Paper, Crown-Zellerbach and Sunbeam in the US, and at Kerry Packer's media empire in Australia. But he was his own worst enemy, once defending his reputation by proclaiming, 'If you want a friend you get a dog'. His downfall came after padding revenues at

Sunbeam and causing a slump in its share price. By comparison, Max Moore-Wilton was a rationalist manager who despite his reputation did grow the business of Sydney Airport Corporation.

It is also in the interests of powerful service providers and advisers, such as lawyers, accountants, brokers, investment bankers and headhunters, to counsel chief executives to pursue a growth strategy. Growth creates fees for these professional firms. By comparison, a company that is returning capital, increasing dividends to shareholders and cutting costs is not generating any fees for service providers and is often labelled as being 'boring' or 'doing nothing'. When you are hiring staff, headhunters earn a success fee of roughly one-third of the new employee's first year's remuneration, but when you sack someone often no professional earns a cent. When I was chief executive I had a banker a week coming to see me with ideas, all of which would have made a lot of money for the bank, but few made sense for Fairfax.

New plant start-ups in which new technologies and equipment are being installed are another example of how the business environment supports a positive bias. I recall a lecture from a visiting professor who argued that new plant rarely earns the returns expected in the early years. Because management is advised by technical experts and suppliers only on the benefits of the new plant, it underestimates the operational difficulties typically faced in the first eighteen months. I learned this lesson with the commissioning of the Tullamarine printing press. Everything that goes wrong during commissioning is happening for the first time; therefore, dealing with the first breakdown of a type may take hours, whereas the second time may only take ten minutes. I took my wife for a late-night visit to Fairfax's new plant after a night out in Melbourne only to find that the presses were not working. Although Claire complained about the heat inside the plant, it was not until two hours had passed that technicians realised the air conditioning had broken down and that the heat had caused computers to fail. Once the temperature was lowered, the problem was fixed. If it had happened again it would probably have taken only fifteen minutes to repair.

Politicians also apply pressure on chief executives to avoid unpopular negative actions. When banks close branches or telcos remove phone booths from country towns local communities are understandably angry. If the anger is being vented in a marginal or swinging seat then politicians get nervous and apply pressure on companies to review their actions. For example, Australia's major telco, Telstra, announced plans to cut 5000 of its 32000 payphones over five years in a bid to cut costs ahead of its full privatisation. After being summoned to a meeting of government senators, Telstra chief executive Sol Trujillo was forced to recant and announced he would not remove any payphones that would jeopardise the health and safety of communities.

There are positive and negative aspects of every management challenge but it is the unseen or ignored negatives that are most likely to inhibit the achievement of sustained good performance. Not only are negatives harder to see, but even when we do see them for what they are emotional barriers stop us from acting on them effectively.

Seeing no evil

Encouraging people to see the negative issues facing an organisation is difficult, particularly when they are doing a good job. A common criticism from Fairfax's senior journalists when I explained why editorial costs needed to be cut was that more — not less — editorial was needed, or the franchise would be ruined. I argued that if the revenue base could not support the cost of editorial and nothing was done, then control of the company would be lost. After all, the basic imperative in any public company is to deliver earnings. The counterargument from some highly articulate journalists was that I showed a failure of imagination and had not thought of enough ways to generate revenue in the traditional newspapers. It is a good rhetorical argument but not a valid one. It offers no solution, particularly when not a single classified–dependent broadsheet worldwide had found new revenue to fully compensate for loss of classifieds.

Recent work on perception and bias has highlighted why most of us have trouble seeing negatives. The research, described in *Smart Choices* by Hammond, Keeney and Raiffa, outlined some common psychological traps.[8] Five in particular resonated with my experience at Fairfax: the status quo trap, the sunk cost trap, seeing what you want to see, the overconfidence trap and a focus on dramatic events.

The status quo trap

There is a natural human tendency to expect the status quo to continue or if it is disturbed to see it as temporary and wait for the return of 'the good old days'.

We can all think of companies that held onto their traditional business or products for too long. Eastman Kodak held out against digital cameras to protect its core film and film camera business and is still paying the price. Kodak has a proud tradition in the photographic film and equipment business stretching back to 1878, when it was the first to introduce simple cameras for the lay photographer. So it is not surprising that Kodak felt it could ride out the digital onslaught to its film business; the strategy met with mixed success. By 1994 Kodak stopped production of traditional film cameras in Western markets, closed facilities and slashed its workforce by up to 25 per cent. Although Kodak is now the largest digital camera manufacturer in the US its share price has been in decline since the late 1990s.

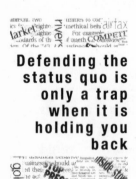

Defending the status quo is only a trap when it is holding you back

Defending the status quo is only a trap when it is holding you back. When the car industry was transformed by a series of mergers and acquisitions in the 1980s and 1990s Toyota stayed with the status quo and made the right decision. Instead of choosing to buy or sell its way out of trouble Toyota chose to continuously improve and innovate, and it became a corporate hero in the process. By contrast, in 1998 Fairfax was in a classic status quo trap, believing that metropolitan newspapers could remain at the core of its business while its competitors diversified into new areas. Kerry Packer's Publishing and Broadcasting Ltd moved into gambling while Rupert Murdoch's News Ltd has moved offshore and into payTV, movies and digital media. Yet despite the need to diversify, the Fairfax board wanted me to defend the status quo and spend more time with journalists!

Work practices at Fairfax were also stuck in a status quo trap. Although *The Australian Financial Review* was willing to change its work practices in order to streamline its operation, the *Herald* and *The Age*, with their strong sense of culture and tradition, held onto the status quo much more stubbornly.

The status quo trap can also apply to decisions about people and processes. It is far easier to give someone whose performance has declined the benefit of the doubt than it is to counsel or sack him or her because he or she is personable, you know the family and hope the worker may return to form given more time.

The sunk cost trap

The second perceptual bias that overemphasises the positive aspects of a situation is the sunk cost trap. The hardest lesson to teach in finance is that sunk costs are no costs. Say you have spent $10 million on a project that still looks uncertain and you are told it will cost $1 million more to make it work. Most people will say you have already spent $10 million so what's one more million to build on your initial investment. However, not spending the

$1 million means you need to confront the negatives of having wasted $10 million. A better way to think about it is that someone has handed you this project for nothing but you have got to spend $1 million to make it work. Framed that way most people would baulk at spending the $1 million. The bottom line is that the project is only worth what you can sell it for, not what you spent on it.

Accounting conventions only serve to support the sunk cost mindset because in accounting you take a write-off for sunk costs that is offset against profits. This makes people think write-offs are an actual cash cost. In reality write-offs are a fiction much like goodwill and amortisation, and most analysts adjust earnings accordingly. Spending money just to avoid a write-off, as some people do, is like throwing good money after bad. When I realised CitySearch was not going to work for Fairfax without spending a lot more time and money developing it I sold the online business to Telstra for about $20 million and took a write-off on the business directory that came with the initial purchase. So although the analysts were valuing CitySearch at nothing, Fairfax earned $20 million from it. This only amounted to about 3¢ a share, but it was a lot better than nothing—and the market gave the decision a big tick despite the fact that the company generated an accounting write-off on the sale.

Seeing what you want to see

Seeing what you want to see stops you seeing negatives when you don't want to acknowledge them. The best Fairfax example was whether a change in the volume of classified employment advertisements was cyclical—that is, part of the normal economic cycle—or structural, with advertisements going to the internet or other forms of print. No-one wanted the problem to be structural because that would require drastic action. So every time there was an upturn in the economy and employment advertising increased, people at Fairfax would say, 'See, there's no structural problem; it's just cyclical and everything will be okay'. All the while Fairfax's classifieds revenue was drifting away to new online competitors, specialist publications, local newspapers and broadcast media.

The corollary to this bias is that people don't see what they don't want to see. Many decent Europeans, for example, failed to see concentration camps in and around their cities and villages. Likewise, traditional bookstores failed to see the threat posed by Amazon and online booksellers. Large chain stores like Borders are surviving by adding coffee shops, holding book readings and meet-the-writer lunches, but small independent bookstores are struggling. Hallmark, as another example, underestimated the threat posed by free e-cards and has resorted to aggressive marketing campaigns to fortify its business.

Although optimism is healthy, psychological studies have shown that pessimists are more realistic. No doubt this was the inspiration behind Intel chief executive Andrew Grove's book, *Only the Paranoid Survive: How to Exploit the Crisis Point that Challenges Every Company*. He argues that to exploit a challenge or crisis from mega-competition, new technology or new regulations you first have to be paranoid about the problem!

Overconfidence trap

My favourite example of the overconfidence trap is that about two-thirds of management students consistently rate themselves in the top third. However, for reckless overconfidence in business it is hard to go past White Star Line, whose 'unsinkable' ship, the *Titanic*, sunk on its maiden voyage with 2300 passengers, yet carried lifeboats for only 962 of them.

There is a good side to overconfidence: it inspires us to tackle difficult challenges and face life with optimism. But it also stops us seeing negatives that we ignore at our peril.

During my time at Fairfax the free *Express* newspaper in Melbourne was launched but Fairfax overestimated the ability of its journalists to produce a lively tabloid. The team assembled from *The Age* was steeped in the traditions of a quality broadsheet, but it was so enthusiastic and full of confidence about the project that I too fell into the overconfidence trap. Another example from my time at Fairfax was the company's attitude to online employment site, Seek. I knew Seek was not prepared to sell its business to Fairfax, but until the day I left the internet team was saying that Seek could be overtaken with organic growth—and I almost believed it. In hindsight I should have seen that classifieds tend to gravitate to the leading site in any category because it is easier to have all buyers and sellers in one place. Therefore, I should have done something other than try to compete head-to-head.

Focus on dramatic events

When statistics and trends are negative, we often seize on a single dramatic event to convince ourselves otherwise; for example, newspaper circulations have been declining slowly but steadily for over twenty years. Yet when Princess Diana died in a car crash in August 1997 circulation of the *Herald* and *The Age* went through the roof. That was the last time that a single event sent newspaper sales rocketing.

There were many major stories over my seven years, including the war in Iraq and the World Trade Center bombing, but none shifted papers like the death of Diana. However, editorial optimists locked onto the Princess Di phenomenon and argued that if only Fairfax could get more stories like that one, circulation would increase, advertisers would flock back to us and the cost pressure would disappear. What people constantly overlook is the rarity of the event, and that an unusual, dramatic event is not necessarily a guide to the future.

Acting on the negatives

Many gardeners are happy to plant and harvest, but very few like to do the pruning and replanting that ensures optimum growth. GE's Jack Welch, who took the ageing industrial conglomerate all the way to number one during his twenty years at the helm, was famous for knowing when and where to prune. If an operation was not performing—which he defined as being number one, two or three in its market—it had to be fixed, sold or closed. He approached staff performance appraisals with similar rigour. Each year the bottom 10 per cent of managers was culled and the top 20 per cent rewarded with 'cash and plaques'. The middle 70 per cent were given honest feedback on how they could improve. The lesson here is that chief executives are just as likely to be undone by a failure to prune as a failure to plant.

Some companies sow the seeds of their own downfall, unaware that they've planted a weed that should be rooted out. Australia's monopoly wheat exporter, AWB, is a good example. AWB allegedly paid $290 million in illegal kickbacks to Saddam Hussein's Iraqi regime under the United Nations's oil-for-food program, defrauding the UN and violating sanctions. During the 2006 government inquiry it became clear that people within the company, the Australian Government, the UN, the US Government and AWB's competitors knew about the kickbacks. However, AWB management was so convinced that it was acting in the best interests of the company, the country and Australian wheat growers that it failed to act on accusations that had the power to undermine its efforts. AWB's corporate standing and its share price suffered, senior managers resigned and future wheat contracts to Iraq were jeopardised.

Seeing a problem is one thing, doing something about it is another. Even when clear-sighted chief executives see the need for negative action, such as selling a division, cutting costs, retrenching staff, or dealing with an underperforming colleague, their emotional make-up can make it difficult to act effectively. This is because these tasks force chief executives to confront people, traditional values or his or her own mistakes — and each has its own difficulties and emotional components.

Confronting people

One of the processes I found hardest to introduce at Fairfax was performance reviews. Done well, they provide formal and informal continuous feedback. Done badly, there is a potential for dysfunctional confrontation. Most people like feedback about their performance but it can be difficult giving negative feedback to loyal staff, many of whom become friends. It's also difficult for them to receive it — especially if performance discussions are not a part of the organisation's culture. Even when the message is negative, clear and accurate feedback is necessary if you want to get the best out of people. In his book *Execution: The Discipline of Getting Things Done* Honeywell chair Larry Bossidy refers to candid dialogue as the 'live ammo' in the people process.[9]

An effective performance review can completely change an underperformer's behaviour

At McKinsey & Co. performance reviews are ongoing and based on the premise that without feedback you can't improve your performance. At Fairfax many of the editorial staff were suspicious of the concept of individual performance management. It was seen as the thin end of the wedge, namely, that it would reduce security of employment and open the way for performance-based pay — which it did.

Yet an effective performance review can completely change an underperformer's behaviour. The review need not take long or be formal. One of my best examples involved a senior manager at Fairfax who was handing me reports late and full of errors. We had a twenty-minute conversation and it never happened again. He said it was the first time anyone had ever pointed out what was expected of him.

The difficulty for managers conducting performance reviews is that everyone they review will act differently and there is seldom any training given to help deal with the problems that can arise. Some senior staff can be very good at selling themselves, creating psychological and emotional barriers in their manager that prevent him or her from saying 'no' or 'not good enough'. Other people underestimate their abilities. I had to explain to one manager what he was good at, what he was not good at, and therefore why he wasn't a good fit for our company. He nearly hugged me and left soon after to do what he did best. We remained friends and he made enough money to buy much better wine for our dinners together than he could afford previously. In another case I suggested slightly altering the role of a promising young manager I had probably promoted too quickly. Two days later he came back and said he had not been able to sleep for dwelling on our conversation and did I want him to go. It took two or three meetings to settle him down. Because you are dealing with people's egos you can get unexpected reactions. I didn't approach that review as well as I should have, but if I was clumsy then more junior managers would have been even clumsier, because I had been holding performance reviews in my different roles for about thirty years.

Even when performance reviews and terminations are well handled there will be cases where people who leave remain bitter and the chief executive is characterised as a rat. I've learned that this just goes with the territory.

While I reviewed people reporting directly to me, they were supposed to review everyone reporting to them, and so on down the line. I brought in a trainer to teach people how to conduct a review because there are certain principles that are helpful and can be taught. Talk about the task—not the person—and be specific.

So rather than say, 'I don't think you're very good at this', it is preferable to phrase the statement this way: 'In that aspect of the job I don't think we are getting results we are happy with, what do you think?' Training enables people to role play, which helps because all the theory in the world will not teach you how to deal with people in real situations.

After a few years Fairfax staff began to say performance review was not such a bad process. It did trigger some departures as it is supposed to, but it also helped to make the company's bonus criteria transparent by getting people to agree on goals and targets for the next twelve months. By the time I left, 79 per cent of Fairfax's 4800 full-time Australian employees were being given performance reviews.

Confronting traditional values

When I joined the Australian Graduate School of Management in 1989 it ran a two-year, full-time MBA modelled on those at prestigious schools like Harvard and Wharton. It was largely government funded and quite small. There was no question that the school had to become much larger in order to cover the range of subjects that a top school needed to teach. Some believed that for the school to grow it needed a part-time program that would attract high-potential executives, who would baulk at taking two years out of their career to study full time. But part-time programs were not then seen as having the same status as full-time programs, and in 1989 few top schools had them.

It was a hard slog challenging the status quo. Faculty meetings degenerated into heated discussions over whether part-timers should be able to use the library or attend classes with full-time students. It would have been far easier and more popular for me to say I wanted to raise a couple of million dollars to double the number of full-time students, but that would have been the wrong thing to do. Ultimately, if the school hadn't confronted the value traditionally placed on full-time MBAs and introduced a part-time program, the school would not be the pre-eminent management school it is today.

At Fairfax I was also forced to confront traditional values. When I arrived in 1997, new to the business and knowing nothing about it, I asked for market research to give me some understanding of what readers thought of Fairfax. The table in my office was piled high with reports, but they were all about specific issues such as what readers thought of the racing form guide or of a new health section. I, by comparison, wanted to know what would make someone who didn't buy the *Herald* take money out of his or her pocket to buy it, or if someone had stopped buying it, why? The assumption was that people wanted the paper. Therefore Fairfax only had to ask whether they wanted it with fries or tabasco, berries or cream; not, do customers want this meal, is it nutritious and do they have time to eat it? The circulation figures told the company nothing about its readers. Readership surveys covered whether readers were male or female, young or old, wealthy or not, but they didn't tell Fairfax why people did or did not buy its papers or why they switched to other publications.

To fix the problem, extensive research was carried out. On the whole editors responded well to improvements in market intelligence and necessary changes were made, both to the papers themselves and to how they were sold and marketed.

Perhaps traditions at Fairfax were so entrenched and so difficult to change because they had never been rigorously questioned or held up to scrutiny.

Confronting your own mistakes

The environment of a public company is tough. Your ego is on the line and one of the toughest emotional challenges is confronting your own mistakes in the full glare of public scrutiny. First you have to be able to acknowledge to yourself that you have made a mistake. Even if you admit it to yourself privately, it is hard to take remedial action when you perceive that investors are just waiting for you to slip up so they can call for your resignation and the appointment of a new chief executive.

A difficulty with the way the market works is that brokers and hedge fund managers make money out of share-price volatility. If there is a crisis and a chief executive is replaced shares drop in price; when a new person is appointed the shares shoot up again. Traders make money on both the decline and rise—so, in the short term, the exit of a chief executive is in their best interest.

I had to confront a number of my mistakes at Fairfax and each time I took corrective action, for example, to wind up an internet site or small publications that didn't work as hoped, the board was supportive. The analysts, however, were quick to start a chorus of 'this bloke's hopeless; he doesn't know what he's doing; he comes up with bad ideas; look at what Hilmer's forays into the internet cost the company'.

In short, dealing with negatives is hard. Hard because negatives are often difficult to see and identify and hard because, even when identified, most of us have to overcome emotional barriers to deal effectively with negative situations. This aversion to negative actions is not just a phenomenon affecting turnaround situations, such as at Fairfax. The problem is as prevalent in high flyers such as Macquarie Bank, Microsoft, Sony or Apple.

Indeed it was my experience of dealing with negatives that gave additional meaning to the title of my introduction, 'On becoming a rat'. But taking negative actions, such as tough people decisions, downsizing or selling, need not entail rat-like behaviour in the unpleasant sense of the word. Negatives can be handled constructively, and the next chapter discusses ways to do this.

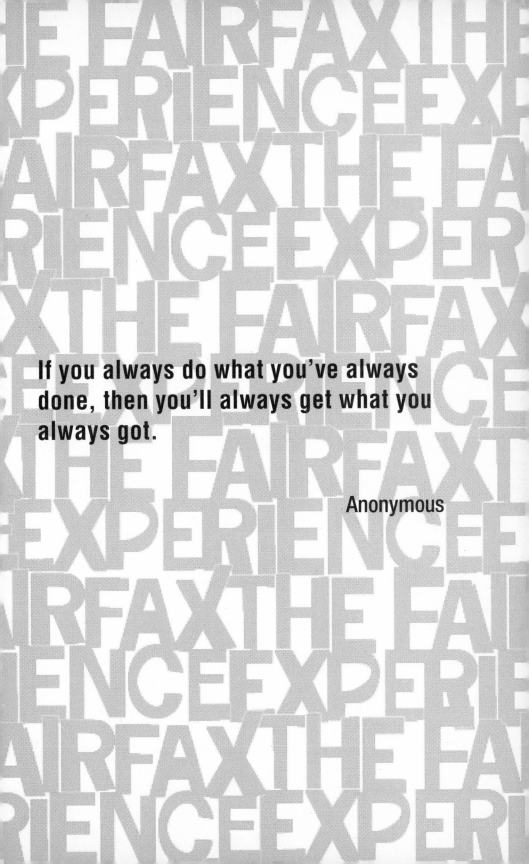

If you always do what you've always done, then you'll always get what you always got.

Anonymous

Chapter 6

 Being positive about
negatives

Imagine that you are selling a mature product or service in an intensely competitive market with little or no growth. You are dependent on a large skilled workforce so labour costs are high. You are also dependent on purchased commodities and under pressure to keep investing big dollars just to hold your position. In other words, you are in the car business in the late 1980s; for argument's sake, suppose you are Toyota.

Faced with these conditions, Toyota had four options. The first was to expand via acquisition into other geographic areas or products to achieve economies of scale and scope. During the late 1980s General Motors went down this path when it took control of Sweden's Saab and a chunk of Japan's Isuzu. Likewise, Chrysler bought American Motors and Ford acquired Jaguar, Volvo, Land Rover and a minority stake in Mazda of Japan. Then in the 1990s Volkswagen bought Britain's Rolls-Royce & Bentley, and BMW bought the Rolls-Royce car marque and Britain's Rover Group.

Toyota's second option was to add new models and push for organic growth. This was the strategy pursued with great fanfare and showmanship by Chrysler's Lee Iaccoca. He was committed to blitzing the market with new models, exciting dealers and selling his way to success. However, success was elusive — in 1998 Chrysler fell to Daimler-Benz, the maker of Mercedes-Benz.

Both of these strategies — expansion via acquisition and the pursuit of organic growth — are positive solutions that completely disregard the negative industry conditions that caused the carmakers' problems (namely high costs, poor process and lack of market understanding).

A third strategy open to Toyota was to quit the business. This strategy is sometimes referred to as the greater fool theory because it assumes there is always a greater fool out there willing to pay your price. Saab, Jaguar and Rover all chose the exit route, leaving their acquirers to battle it out with the competition with mixed success.

A fourth option for Toyota was to cut costs and improve quality by pursuing a systematic, long-term strategy. No takeovers or miracle cures, just patient execution, rigorous professionalism and a dash of innovation. As each target is met, another is set. It is what Toyota did and continues to do with great success.

These last two strategies recognise the negatives. Quitting the business is often a good strategy, although few people become heroes doing it. Certainly the studies on takeovers show that shareholders in target companies generally emerge as the winners. However, employees in target companies often end up without jobs unless the new owner chooses to reinvigorate the business. This happened when Rupert Murdoch's News Ltd sold the INL business to Fairfax. The takeover created a situation in which employees had the choice of joining Fairfax or taking a redundancy package. A percentage did opt for redundancy, and when Fairfax took over it discovered that the business could be operated and even expanded with the smaller staff numbers. Moreover, the employees who remained could begin working for an owner who was committed to the business.

The Toyota way

Toyota chose not to sell but instead to deal with the negative environment in a positive way by attending to what I refer to as the four P's—perception, persistence, people and persuasion.

Toyota saw clearly what needed to be done to trade its way out of trouble, even though the prospect was daunting. Unlike many of its peers in the car industry Toyota did not fall into the perceptual trap of thinking that the problems in the car industry were temporary or simply part of the normal business cycle. It also did not delude itself into believing that other carmakers had been luckier with new models and that it would be Toyota's turn next.

Toyota saw clearly what needed to be done to trade its way out of trouble, even though the prospect was daunting

Once Toyota identified a solution it showed extraordinary persistence in sticking to its plan. The Toyota production system (TPS) and its emphasis on Kaizen—continuous improvement of products and services—is

one of the longest adhered-to strategies in corporate history. It aims to position Toyota as a leader in both quality and cost efficiency—ideas that were once considered incompatible but are now seen as potentially complementary. The Toyota system relies on the rigorous application of principles and practices, including just-in-time delivery of parts to the production line; not allowing a defect to carry over from one machine to the next; and lean manufacturing (the reduction of waste to improve the quality of everything from production and waiting times to transportation and inventory). Far from being timid due to its position in a troubled industry, Toyota also took calculated risks with innovative technology. Indeed, the carmaker was the first to experiment with hybrid technology, which it installed in its Prius model back in 1997.

Toyota also dealt with people skilfully, achieving productivity gains by keeping its employees on side. Where other carmakers slashed their workforce to cut costs, Toyota showed a preference for retraining and redeployment and a willingness to use the knowledge and expertise of its workforce. The carmaker empowered people by allowing any worker to stop the production line if he or she detected a fault.

The fourth piece of the strategy was persuasion. Toyota was remarkably open about its strategy and its trend-setting production system, communicating clearly with employees, customers, governments and the market. Toyota told the world it was going to make better cars cheaper every year; unlike the mission statements released by many other companies, Toyota actually delivered on its pledge.

Not surprisingly, many companies have tried to emulate Toyota but none has used its methods so successfully. General Motors learned a lot from the Saturn plant in California, which it operates jointly with Toyota, but it could not replicate Saturn's success at its other American plants. Even though Saturn churned out identical cars badged either as GM or Toyota, a Boston Consulting Group study found that the Toyota cars had a greater resale value due to consumer confidence in the company's dealer and service network.[10]

Despite fierce competition among carmakers, Toyota continues to outperform its competition in technological innovation, customer satisfaction, continuous growth and profit. By 2005 Toyota was the tenth-largest company in the world and one of the top three car manufacturers.

The Fairfax dilemma

The Toyota solution of a multi-decade commitment to quality and cost leadership is not for everyone—and it did not fit the situation at Fairfax. The car business might have been troubled, but it did have underlying growth in demand. By contrast, classified-dependent metro newspapers worldwide were losing circulation and ad volumes and had been doing so for at least twenty years. Nor did Fairfax have decades to transform the business, like Toyota did. Instead the board wanted a quick fix and gave me twelve months to cut $40 million from the cost base. So I achieved the cost-cutting target quickly and then searched for opportunities to fortify its core newspaper business. Unfortunately, the prospects for growing the business were limited. The company looked at expanding into other geographical areas by taking *The Age* to Adelaide and starting a weekly review newspaper in other states, but competitors already occupied the ground and advertisers were not interested. So Fairfax innovated at the margins, with new colour magazines and inserts. However, a successful add-on publication will only add a few million dollars in profit—the company, by contrast, had hundreds of millions at risk.

To make matters worse, I found no media model for a broadsheet, classified-dependent newspaper organisation that would pull me out of the hole I found myself in at Fairfax. London's Daily Mail Company is the best newspaper example of a business 'doing a Toyota' by sticking to its knitting. Daily Mail knew its market very well. It also innovated and marketed aggressively and defied the circulation trends better than most, but it did not have Fairfax's classifieds problem. Likewise, The Washington Post Company and Thomson had diversified out of newspapers, but Fairfax was not in a position to do that. Cross-media ownership laws prevented expansion into broadcasting, and the company could not follow The Washington Post Company's large-scale entry into education because Australia did not have a large private education sector to invest in.

One of the disadvantages of not having an owner-shareholder is that it is far more difficult to move into new fields. Institutional shareholders are reluctant to support such moves, especially those by a relatively inexperienced chief executive. The owner-shareholders, such as the Packers, Rupert Murdoch and Kerry Stokes, had both the position and experience to bring their shareholders along with them as they expanded into new fields; whereas I had neither the reputation nor the ego to say, 'Give me a few billion dollars and I'll make money for you'. From the institutions' perspective, buying a share in Fairfax and a share in gaming group Tabcorp would entail less risk than supporting a Fairfax move into gambling via acquisition of Tabcorp. So instead of risking its shareholders' funds on takeovers in new areas, the company saw positive potential in regional and community newspapers and the internet, and it used money generated by the metros to fund acquisitions in these areas.

I looked around the world but did not see a major broadsheet with a solution

At Fairfax the management team was constantly confronted with the realisation that the negative aspects of the company's situation were worse than any positive opportunities being considered. The team dealt with the negatives by cost cutting, and it searched for positives with moderate success. I looked around the world but did not see a major broadsheet with a solution.

The media industry was not the only industry dealing with the negatives of a product in terminal decline—the automobile industry was suffering too. The lesson for me from Toyota, a company I greatly admire, and my own experience in the chief executive's role is not to 'stick to your knitting'. Instead, the lesson is about how to reframe the negatives in a positive light (a subject that few textbooks cover well but one that is worth exploring).To do this, a chief executive must keep Toyota's four P's—perception, persistence, people and persuasion—in mind when tackling the negatives.

Perception

The first problem I had to rectify at Fairfax was the narrow and blinkered way people perceived the problems afflicting the company and the newspaper industry in general. In chapter 5 I discuss some common perceptual barriers to effective management. The status quo trap, seeing what you want to see, the sunk cost trap, overconfidence and a focus on dramatic but improbable events had infected Fairfax, and I was not immune.

If you believe the status quo will continue, that your problems are temporary and that newspapers will continue to produce their rivers of gold, then you act as Fairfax had in the past. It means you invest in new printing presses, upgrade infrastructure, move into expensive office space and fly business class. You also tend to stick with businesses that are not working, such as the CitySearch directory business (to use an example from Fairfax). The status quo is embedded in the organisation—that the business might not be sustainable is not an idea the people around you want you to contemplate. The chief executive treads a fine line when suggesting the old business model has a limited future because this can easily become a self-fulfilling prophecy and erode public and staff confidence in the company. It was an argument levelled at me both from within and outside Fairfax when I started cutting costs and reducing staff numbers.

Unless you can break through the perceptual barriers and see what is really going on, you have no hope of dealing with the negatives. After all, seeing is a precondition for taking correct action. The chief executive's dilemma, however, is that an organisation that is continually questioning, studying, discussing and searching for possible insights into trends is unlikely to move forward effectively and aggressively.

Most of what goes on in an organisation is about doing, not endless questioning. Strategising and committing to a longer term course of action are central to a chief executive's job, but so are execution and building, and leading an effective, motivated team. At Fairfax, although there were fundamental threats to the business that needed to be perceived and understood, the company still had newspaper businesses that would likely continue for decades, and which needed to be well run and continuously trimmed and improved.

The right question

I soon reached the view that the way through the perception traps was not to approach a company like a university, where questioning and research is the way of life. Fairfax needed to get on with the job while also creating opportunities for reflection that would challenge and punctuate assumptions from time to time. I needed to create a culture that could handle these situations without paralysing the business or demotivating staff.

The starting point for generating this space, and it is very much a chief executive's responsibility, is to ask the right question. One of my favourite sayings is 'The answer is in the question'. Think about the implication of identifying the key question for Fairfax in 1998 as, 'How can $40 million be cut from the cost base?' The question assumes the business is fine, just inefficient, and it drives behaviour accordingly. But with my reputation on the line and the chair's public pledge, I had to accept the task I was given.

Even McKinsey & Co., with its status as a top management-consultancy group, fell into the trap of answering the wrong question about Fairfax. It focused entirely on cost reduction, rather than raising the more challenging issues threatening Fairfax's future and insisting the company face them.

Cutting costs may have been necessary but it wasn't sufficient to put Fairfax on track for sustainable growth. The retort to 'How can costs be cut by $40 million?' could have been 'Even if $40 million is cut, does Fairfax then have a credible strategy for sustainable growth?'—and the answer would have been obvious. Warren Buffett has a great question that is as relevant to a chief executive as it is to an investor: 'Would I buy the business I'm in for the price it currently trades at?' If not, some major rethinking is needed. Once again, the answer is in the question.

As chief executive, how do you ensure you ask the right question even if it happens to be an awkward one? A part of being able to ask these types of questions springs from human nature. Some people, like Andy Grove at Intel and Frank Lowy at Westfield, are inveterate and persistent questioners.

The corporate cocoon

I found that as CEO, to ask the right questions I needed ways to break out of the corporate cocoon. It is easy for chief executives to live in hermetically sealed comfort zones. My travel was handled seamlessly — cars, special airport lounges and first class seating (even when I booked economy) were organised for me in advance. My lunch would appear if I wasn't going out. People would rearrange their schedules to fit mine — quite the opposite to my previous roles, in which I would be the one adjusting my schedule. Much of this makes sense, however, given the time pressures and the confidential nature of most of the meetings and conversations I was having.

Yet as chief executive, a more dangerous part of the comfort zone is that you also have a large number of people whose jobs and career prospects are heavily dependent on you. It is therefore natural that people are trying to guess what you are thinking and what you want done. When the company is on the right track and the main challenge is to execute well, having a team keen to accomplish what the chief executive wants to do is a real plus. It is not about being surrounded by 'yes men', which I think is always a risk, but about having a team that can do and wants to do things according to a well-understood strategy.

Although the cocoon makes sense in some circumstances, it can cause real problems in perception. Bad news has trouble penetrating the corporate cone of silence. I recall a story I heard about one chief executive who was about to attend a conference with key staff. That morning the press had printed a critical article about him and the company. How was this handled? The keepers of his cocoon collected and removed all the copies of the paper from the conference venue! At Fairfax I was constantly frustrated by people hiding bad news in the hope that they could fix the problem before I heard about it, or that the difficulty would resolve itself in time.

There are a number of ways to escape the cocoon from time to time to get a fresh view, something that is critical in avoiding the perception traps. The first is to have a few people on the management team who are natural sceptics — those who are not afraid to question the chief executive and board. In this respect I was well served by two chief financial officers, Sankar Narayan and Mark Bayliss. This fundamental questioning is, in my view, as important a part of a chief financial officer's role as producing accounts, raising money and providing information.

Analysts and institutional shareholders can also stimulate fresh ideas. Some of the most thought-provoking and challenging questions about the business came from foreign-based institutional analysts. Australian analysts, with few exceptions, were too focused on the short term and in trying to accurately pick the company's next reported earnings. When I travelled overseas and visited the big investment houses I would often come away energised because they really made you think. Because they invested in media in a number of countries, they knew the business well and asked insightful questions, such as how to make the business less cyclical and how to change the revenue base. They looked at the long-term questions, rather than the short-term ones, such as asking if I thought the enterprise bargaining agreement would cost another 3 or 5 per cent the following year. Even on editorial matters the overseas analysts asked better questions than the local ones, about the company's market research and what it showed about readers.

Customers, front-line employees, bankers, consultants, family and friends with an interest in the business and what you are doing are also helpful in getting more accurate and challenging perceptions through the corporate cocoon. As chief executives live in an environment of imperfect information and need to act before a trend is widely apparent, having networks that tell you what is or may be going on is critical. This is one advantage of managers who grow up in an industry. The flip side, however, and where I believed I had an advantage, was that neither I nor people in my network were so wedded to newspapers that we couldn't see the threats.

Having networks that tell you what is or may be going on is critical

One of the roles that boards of directors are supposed to play is to ask the big questions and challenge the status quo. The Fairfax board, however, had difficulties with this role. Although there were a number of directors of great ability whose private counsel was extremely valuable, the board did not function effectively in formal meetings. Minor issues too readily dominated the agenda and interpersonal relationships among directors were often difficult. Although shareholders understood the board had problems, I did not agree with what was proposed as the solution — namely, more directors with industry experience. Fairfax had plenty of industry experience on the board. What it lacked was a composition of minds that could work collegially and be able to ask and follow through on the big questions constructively.

Boards can play this critical role, as I learned from my experience at Westfield, Foster's and Macquarie Bank. However, research suggests that effective boards — those that question and stimulate strategy — are the exception.

A dynamic culture

In any organisation it is proper from time to time to question the basis of the business. But unless there is a culture that encourages this, starting at the top, the clear and timely perception of threats and even opportunities is impossible.

Early in my career at McKinsey & Co. I was asked to review the strategy of W. R. Carpenter Ltd. Carpenters was a well-established Pacific trading company with interests in plantations, shipping and trading commodities. I concluded that this kind of business had little future, although parts of it were sound. A deconstruction and reconstruction was required. When I explained this to the chair he took the report out of my hands and tore it in half; but his company went the way of the merchant clippers.

The weight of history can sink a business that is not willing to adjust to new circumstances, but there are also times when a culture of respecting the company's history is important. An appreciation of the lessons of the past can be especially helpful in avoiding the overconfidence trap. I was at a disadvantage at Fairfax because I had no history in the company or the newspaper industry. So when the company built a new printing plant I was not aware of the potential traps. Peter Graham, who was in charge of the project, spent a lot of time speaking to people who had been involved with the installation of the Chullora printing plant seven years earlier. Although that project had not been handled well, after staff members were fully debriefed the company was able to avoid repeating earlier mistakes. (Management used to say, for example, that the Chullora plant was not just at the leading edge but at the 'bleeding edge' of new technology. Likewise, if the Chullora mail room, which automatically assembled the sections into one paper, broke down there was no manual backup and the whole production stopped.) Because the company recognised these problems in its history, when the Tullamarine plant was built Fairfax adopted a policy of only using proven technologies.

Another aspect of having a dynamic culture is to value learning and training. When I started at Fairfax, training was nonexistent outside technical areas. This changed over time, as would be expected from a company with a chief executive with my background in education. Sending key people on training and fact-finding missions overseas also helped to perceive what was going on more clearly. Tom Burton, one of Fairfax's most experienced senior journalists, attended a program at the Kellog School in Chicago, which dealt provocatively with the challenges facing broadsheets. And Alan Revell and Darren Challis's visits to various players in the emerging digital business produced not only a strategic direction but also some specific opportunities the company could pursue.

Consultants and good moderators of conferences can also help a team develop a culture that balances execution of strategy with questioning and perceiving accurately. However, the success of consultants or moderators is limited by the degree to which the chief executive supports them. In other words, without clear briefs and agendas and a willingness from top management to listen, these exercises are a waste of time.

Persistence

During my seven years at Fairfax the strategy evolved but remained essentially consistent. Early on I was required to carry out a number of negative acts and decisions, such as cost cutting and selling businesses (in fact the first real decision I made was to sell Australian Geographic). Decisions to sell are generally unpopular so you need courage, strength of character and a thick skin to weather the inevitable backlash from critics.

Something I did not realise from outside the business was how resilient I needed to become if I was to move forward and not be diverted from Fairfax's goals. One of the competitive tools in the media industry is to destabilise the competition with distorted coverage of their actions. After the crash of high-tech stocks I was painted in rival media reports as the last believer in the internet. I'm proud to wear that mantle now, but at the time it was intended as a derisory remark. Indeed, I believe Fairfax's ultimate success with the internet was a mark of my persistence.

During my time at McKinsey I worked with Bob Waterman, co-author of *In Search of Excellence*, on a project to discover why some mineral exploration companies find new mines and others don't. We collected data from companies on their exploration programs, targets and budgets. Success could not be explained by spending because the biggest spenders often found fewer mines. Ultimately, success came down to clarity of target and the length of time companies persisted with their exploration. Unsuccessful explorers had on–again off–again budgets, while successful ones had consistent spending irrespective of the commodity cycle. The reason for this is that once you cut back spending, key people are lost. Then when the cycle turns up and the budget increases, new people need to be hired and retrained. This incurs costs in time and results in lost experience. We also found that successful explorers spent more of their budgets on drilling holes than on desk research. The lesson we took away was that learning by trial and experiment goes hand in hand with persistence. The parallel at Fairfax was to stick with the internet and keep trying new ideas, despite the criticism.

As a chief executive you must be able to deal with the glare of public criticism. A *Bulletin* article by journalist and ex-*Herald* editor John Lyons suggested I was an idiot for buying INL in New Zealand, while Mark Westfield at Rupert Murdoch's *The Australian* criticised me for almost everything I did. Luckily I was at a good point in my life—being late in my career and with a strong support network of family and friends—to be able to deal with the onslaught. I made light of such press reports with my management team, who referred to *The Bulletin* as 'the government in exile' because it was staffed by ex-Fairfax people pining for the day Kerry Packer would buy Fairfax and they could return to power. The Packer journalists also fell into the trap of believing what they wanted to see, namely, that Fairfax was incapable of getting anything right. I argued that it was good that News Ltd was attacking the company because it indicated Fairfax was getting under the media player's skin and being taken seriously.

As a chief executive you must be able to deal with the glare of public criticism

When Rupert Murdoch wrote me a personal letter saying Fairfax coverage of his family was beneath contempt, I let a number of people see it. I was not going to be browbeaten by that sort of pressure. A lesson I learned from *Herald* war correspondent Paul McGeough was not to give your critics oxygen. I refused to let my agenda be driven by critics and often did not even bother to read offending articles. I also never took legal action over defamatory comments about me, unlike Kerry Packer, who, as I mentioned earlier, once sued me personally over a comment by a columnist in the *Herald*. In the end he lost and I insisted that Fairfax's legal team be paid its costs.

I learned a lot about myself during these episodes. First, I realised that as CEO, no matter what I felt about critical reports in our competitors' press, it was essential that I indicate through my demeanour and actions that those reports are irrelevant, and that Fairfax knew what it was doing and would continue along that path. Second, I quickly learned to ignore these reports. Lack of self-confidence has not been a problem for me, something I found to be an important attribute when under attack.

In short, I learned to make light of irrational and ill-informed criticism, to deny critics oxygen and to shun unnecessary public attention. You need a good support structure to do this, to surround yourself with people of quality and integrity whom you respect and who encourage you to ignore critics and persist with your game plan. The final lesson is to stay focused and know where you want to go.

People

Many of the negatives a chief executive has to deal with involve removing, disciplining or even demoting people, and much of the negative publicity stems from this issue. As discussed earlier, 'Chainsaw' Al Dunlap earned his nickname because of his reputation for ruthlessly slashing staff numbers and closing operations, but his methods are of limited use. In fact, they tend to cause more problems than they solve. Dealing effectively with people when you have to deliver a negative message is a critical skill for strong managers.

The starting point is to understand that life does not end for someone who is fired or made redundant, especially in a buoyant economy. Yet firing someone can sometimes feel like a reflection of your own failure, either in wrongly hiring or promoting the person in the first place or in not developing them. This can lead to a self-protective mechanism whereby you convince yourself the person you fired was hopeless. Employees can also develop a protective wall, believing a colleague was fired because the boss was an idiot. I believe Fairfax handled negative people decisions quite well. Although I turned over almost the entire top management team, there was none of the drama, court action and press reports that occurred at the Packer-controlled Channel 9. Nor did Fairfax's stars defect to our competitors.

A second guideline for effectively handling personnel negatives is to treat people with respect. At McKinsey I was taught that firing someone is never about an employee's intrinsic worth, it is about understanding and discussing the fit between the person's skills and interests and the organisation's needs. A number of the people I was forced to retrench went on to better jobs and remained friends with me. There is no joy in psychologically hurting a person you fire and focusing on 'fact and fit' helps you avoid this. If you haven't got the stomach for these conversations then you won't make an effective senior manager. Remember that voluntary redundancies give people a chance to make their own decisions, which is a preferable course of action when a number of people need to be retrenched.

Treating people with respect starts with conversations based on fact and business issues—not whether the employee is a 'good' or 'bad' person. The timing and the words used should also be chosen carefully. I never announced redundancies or fired someone just before Christmas because he or she would face weeks when few jobs are advertised and the experience would destroy the family holiday. People often say or do things they later regret when they are fired so it is cruel to do the deed at 11.00 in the morning, when the office is packed. It is better to have the discussion at the end of the day so that the person affected can go home and reflect on his or her next move. Some people choose to work out their contract, whereas others want to leave immediately. I tried to accommodate employee wishes as far as possible.

Treating people with respect is important not just because it is an ethical and humane way to act. When cuts are made and people are fired everyone in the organisation is watching. If these events are handled badly, the employees who stay conclude that this could happen to them; loyalty and enthusiasm suffer and good people may become demotivated or leave.

Thought should also be given to who needs to be informed about your decision. When I intended firing a senior staff member I discussed it with the chair rather than the board members. In a leaky organisation you increase the risk of sensitive information being revealed inadvertently, and I didn't want people to hear of their own sacking on the grapevine. I also discussed any senior firing with the head of human resources and the communications manager because the exit of a senior manager often needs to be reported to the stock exchange. I generally had a news release drafted beforehand that I would let the person concerned check and suggest any alternative wording he or she would be more comfortable with. Fairfax also gave outplacement support after the event to help people find jobs. Most executives get six to twelve months pay in these circumstances depending on length of service and the details of their contract. It is crucial that the firing or retrenchment process is handled swiftly, or it will be leaked in a gossip column before you are prepared for it.

Although it is important to handle people with respect, the chief executive must be tough when necessary. I had one staff member dismissed on the spot, for example, for hacking into my email. People said I was harsh, that he had apologised, but I believed the company had to dismiss him. Someone in advertising who was abusing his power to give discounts to customers also had to be dismissed quickly.

Persuasion

Dealing effectively with employees and getting your message across require good communication skills and the ability to persuade people to support the direction you are taking. The first lesson I learned about the need to communicate my strategy to Fairfax staff and the investment community was that whatever time I spent on communication it was never enough. Many people did not fully understand the strategy—sometimes wilfully but usually because I, and my management team, did not spend enough time on persuasion. This was due partly to my dislike for endless meetings, but it is no excuse. The second lesson I learned was that I did not push my team hard enough to communicate down the line. In other words, the whole organisation needs to be involved in communicating your objectives. Effective communication within a business is a two-way street that involves both listening and talking.

Management textbooks on communication report that the further removed people are from the boss the less credibility the boss has in their eyes. People give most credence to communication from their direct supervisor. People higher up in the organisation are commonly perceived as not only lacking in credibility but distant and inclined to speak in jargon. I could use terms like ROE (return on equity) and TSR (total shareholder return) and be confident that the board would understand. However, if I went to the editorial floor or to one of our printing plants and slipped the same jargon into conversation it would poison communications. This was not generally a problem, though I needed to think about each audience carefully ahead of a meeting.

When you communicate you have to be yourself and your management team has to be in tune with the message. Some senior people would say to my face that they agreed with my direction and then do the opposite. If you can see that someone does not share your vision then you need to either change their views or let them go (again, this is an issue of compatibility, not intrinsic worth).

My third lesson in communication was that words matter, especially in a newspaper company! I made a mistake early on by admitting that I was not an avid reader of newspapers, and that remark came back to haunt me. It was the truth but I was foolishly honest. Content provider was a term I learned to avoid because it was perceived as denigrating the craft of writing (although I had been happy to be referred to as a content provider when writing articles for academic journals). The other phrase that provoked a surprising reaction from staff was 'effective surprise', which meant telling people something they don't already know or hadn't thought about deeply in a way that catches their attention. I said in one meeting that if Fairfax didn't use the concept in its newspapers or websites then the company had failed. It went down like

When you communicate you have to be yourself and your management team has to be in tune with the message

a lead balloon, even though the phrase comes from an important essay on creativity by eminent psychologist Jerome Bruner. I was told that effective surprise essentially meant tabloid journalism and was tantamount to dumbing down content. 'Pruning' was also considered a bad term because it implied dead wood, but 'reinventing' and 'renewing', by contrast, were perceived as good. As I learned, companies and corporate cultures will interpret words in ways that will surprise someone from outside their industry or culture.

My fourth lesson in persuasion was to communicate from the company's core objectives—and my objective was to make Fairfax a strong independent company. Like The Washington Post Company, Fairfax's metropolitan newspapers could be at the core of the company's values without being at the core of its business. Communication should flow from your objectives or goals in a way that people can associate with and take pride in. The idea is captured in the phrase 'Lead from a higher cause'. When I managed to communicate my dedication to pursuing strong journalism and a strong and independent company, it went down well with staff. However, there are times and circumstances where the chief executive needs to be circumspect about strategy for reasons of commerce and staff morale. Towards the end of my tenure I had forty people or so working on a project modelling what would happen to the company's newspapers if classified revenues declined further. All agreed that the business would not be sustainable in its current form and that the company would have to continue shedding staff. Yet I was still reluctant to go to a paper where people were doing their best and say, 'You are all doing a terrific job. How many are here? Two hundred? One hundred and eighty might be about right ... for now'.

Managers who aspire to lead a successful organisation have no choice — they need to be able to tackle the negatives as well as the positives. Yet I believe negatives can be handled without becoming a rat, even if at times you will be called a rat for what you have to do.

The key, as I found not only from my own experience but also from other cases, such as Toyota, is to deal with each of the four P's. Perception is critical because you can't act on what you can't see. Persistence is required because the emotional and political obstacles to taking negative action are greater than when you take positive actions. Self-confidence, a thick skin and a solid support structure are vital. Also, people have to be managed with respect, for their own wellbeing and because the rest of the organisation will judge you by whether, in its eyes, you are fair and respectful to others. Finally, never underestimate the importance and value of time spent on persuasion.

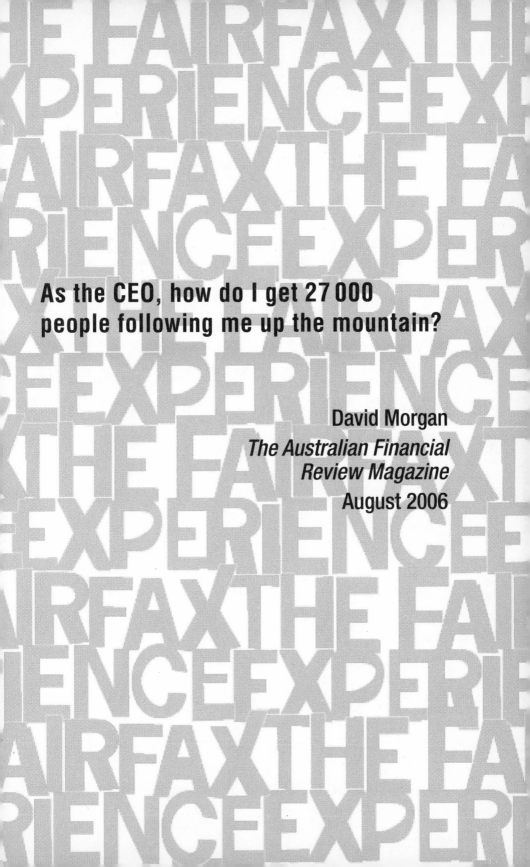

As the CEO, how do I get 27 000
people following me up the mountain?

David Morgan
*The Australian Financial
Review Magazine*
August 2006

Chapter 7

Lessons for leaders and educators

There are two questions that my experience as a chief executive highlighted. First is the one canvassed in numerous bestsellers—namely, what does it take to succeed as a leader of a large, complex enterprise? Second, what are the implications of my experience for management education? In other words, are students being taught the right things in the right way?

Leadership

Leadership is often mentioned but rarely defined. Like reasonableness or pornography, when people come across leadership, in the words of US Supreme Court Justice Potter Stewart, they 'know it when they see it'. When business people nominate effective leaders there tends to be agreement on the names—Michael Chaney, Wesfarmers; Gail Kelly, St George Bank;

and Alan Moss, Macquarie Bank, to name a few. Although most people see leadership in terms of business performance and have less of an awareness or understanding of how leaders operate day-to-day, I believe that leadership, with all its components, can be defined.

For me, leadership is about encouraging and motivating others to change their opinions and actions to challenge their own boundaries. Everyone has aspirations and opinions, and levels of performance that can be reached on his or her own. And many individuals—those referred to and respected as 'driven people'—have high expectations of themselves in this regard. However, most people, even driven people, can have their viewpoint and actions challenged in order to venture beyond their 'comfort zones'—whether it means trying harder, approaching a task differently or taking a more calculated risk. Strong leadership entails having this effect on the people you are responsible for.

Leadership is about encouraging and motivating others to change their opinions and actions to challenge their own boundaries

Leadership means driving others to surpass their usual performance level by altering the momentum and direction of their actions to ensure better results. To use an example from Fairfax, it does not take leadership by an editor-in-chief to release the newspapers on time every day. The default position of the company and its people is to accomplish this task day in and day out—and it invariably happens. The challenge lies in whether Fairfax can put out a newspaper that absorbs and effectively surprises its readers every day. So improving a newspaper—its quality, its effect on its readership and market, its advertiser appeal and how it tackles the threat to its classified advertising—is just one example in which strong leadership makes a real difference to outcomes.

The characteristics of success

As discussed in chapter 2, there is no single, simple answer to the question 'What does it take to succeed as a leader?' But as I struggled with the challenges of the chief executive role, and discussed them with my peers, I came to believe that a number of characteristics are critical. These attributes are not my 'five steps to success'; they are more about the person in a leadership role and how he or she may handle situations. In my view, leadership requires five key attributes — brains, energy, determination, trust and ethics.

Brains

Great leaders have the brainpower to master their business and achieve success. To cut through the noise and chaff that surround and distract people daily, you need the clarity and focus a keen intellect can provide. An ability to see the reality of a situation and prioritise is critical. To be able to identify the tectonic shape of a business — to understand the drivers that affect revenue, profit, cash flow, opportunities and reputation — is the difference between success and mediocrity. In other words, good leaders can separate the signals from the noise.

Whether a culture that recognises and rewards brainpower exists in the business world is another matter. This point hit home when I was completing my Wharton School studies and attending job interviews. One large company asked if I had an objection to completing psychological and intelligence tests. I replied that I had no issue with the requirement provided the psychologist offered feedback. At my debriefing session the psychologist counselled me against a career in line management. Why? I scored too highly on intelligence and, in this company's view, would therefore see too many angles in scenarios I would have to deal with and be indecisive. This perspective exists today. It was portrayed in a review of a book on the CEO of Viacom, Sumner Redstone. Redstone was seen, and often presented himself, as a yokel cinema operator from Boston. In fact he was someone with an exemplary academic record who was driven to build one of the world's pre-eminent entertainment conglomerates.

Although the rags-to-riches stories always attract great attention, most successful chief executives are highly intelligent and have strong academic records — even though discussing it is frowned upon.

Energy

Leadership is neither a part-time nor an armchair activity. Truly great leaders demonstrate high energy levels over long periods of time. Consider Frank Lowy and the continued worldwide expansion of Westfield. When Frank was well into his sixties, I worked with him and his colleagues on the float of Westfield America on the New York Stock Exchange. Working on a global book-building exercise before setting the opening price of the stock, we were in New York the day before the scheduled listing. We received bids from US institutions throughout the day. As night fell the Australian bids came through, and after midnight the European bids too. We had been working for over twenty-four hours in a tense environment, and early in the morning the team members began falling asleep, one person while making notes at his desk. Throughout the night, however, one indivdual kept operating at a high tempo — Frank.

Leaders have to energise their organisations. They do this by example and by inspiring, coaxing and stimulating. Entropy, in my observation, applies to the business world as surely as it does in other spheres. A leader provides extra energy and compensates for the wasted or unavailable energy resulting from a disorderly organisation and haphazard decision making and operating systems. The requirement of high energy in leaders appears to ring true in non-business arenas as well. The Australian Prime Minister, John Howard, for example, is known for the exceptional vigour and physical energy he brings to his role.

Determination

Identifying and then charting a course of action and possessing the energy to pursue it are necessary but not sufficient conditions for strong leadership. Leadership requires having significant determination and willpower—such as that shown by Sumner Redstone. I once attended a speech Redstone gave, and although he was an engaging speaker, I noticed that he had burnt and disfigured hands. Apparently he had been caught in a hotel fire and had clung to an outside ledge until he was rescued; his determination to survive reveals much about his success as a chief executive.

Leaders who want to change the momentum of their organisation or alter its direction often run into opposition. Sometimes this resistance is overt and can be tackled directly. (I certainly had my share of this in press commentary, most notably from competing media companies.) However, resistance is often concealed, framed as helpful advice about why change is inappropriate or why more research and time is needed.

Maintaining a course of action despite resistance requires a strong will. Leaders may have second thoughts and doubts but they cannot and do not reveal them, except perhaps to one or two close confidants. Studies of effective leaders often refer to their resilience, their thick skin in the face of criticism and their ability to determinedly pursue a course of action even when the people around them are unconvinced. Examples of this include the discipline of Wesfarmers in sticking with its investment criteria even though suitable investments may not appear for some years. Similarly, Rio Tinto followed a course of action to create an enterprise-based, flexible and productive work environment in the Pilbara region under three successive leaders—Sir Roderick Carnegie, John Ralph and Leigh Clifford—despite union and government opposition, and significant short-term costs.

Trust

Trust is necessary to gain the confidence of others. Although people can be ordered to do things they would not otherwise do, unless they trust the leader and appreciate the need to work differently, their performance will suffer. The hardest and most important tasks in business today—inventiveness, customer courtesy and going the extra mile to meet a customer's needs—cannot be mandated. In a low- or no-trust environment the penalty is a dysfunctional workforce. This is revealed in the environment created by the Stasi, employed as secret police under East Germany's communist regime. Because East Germany was a low-trust or even a no-trust environment, the government used spying and punishment to keep its citizens in line. According to my calculations, the number of people in the Stasi accounted for about 5 per cent of East Germany's workforce! In other words, in a no-trust environment you can anticipate a 5 per cent 'inefficiency tax' plus a workforce that grudgingly operates at low performance levels.

Ethics

Outstanding leadership also requires a solid ethical or moral position. Essentially, the enterprise should not simply be seen by leaders as just a place to make a dollar, but instead as an enterprise that stands for something important. Also, the company's leaders should be perceived to be doing the right thing—from producing products of quality and value, to providing transparency of actions, to resisting the lure of greed. Ethics underpins trust, and ethical dilemmas are present in business no less than politics or day-to-day life.

Finally, leadership should not be confused with charisma. Although the media spotlight always follows the wealthiest and most powerful

business magnates, effective business leaders do not seek media coverage in the social pages. Indeed, I believe that the courting of media attention is often a sign of impending demise.

Born or made

If these five characteristics are important, then the final question is about how they can be developed and improved. Are leaders born, or are they made? And what is the relative importance of education versus experience?

I believe that all influences that shape a true leader matter. Although people are born with a set of attributes, both education and experience can help shape and improve them. Brainpower or IQ may be largely given, but how you use your brain and supplement natural wit with learning can make a huge difference. For example, what I had learned about accounting and finance—initially as a student and later via practice—was critical to understanding Fairfax's developing priorities.

How you use your brain and supplement natural wit with learning can make a huge difference

Energy and determination may be harder attributes to teach and develop but they are essential for leaders in high-pressure situations. Indeed, I found that environments that required sustained high levels of energy and determination helped improve my capacity. (For me, these situations arose when I had to write or study in 'crisis mode' at university or work to unreasonable deadlines.) In other words, people can improve their capabilities if they are stretched to see what is possible.

Trust and ethics can be taught and should be integral parts of education. Yet these attributes also develop from experience and role models—such as parents, teachers, colleagues and bosses, and leaders in the community.

In summary, the five leadership characteristics I've mentioned can all be improved. Although each of us is born with certain talents that matter, what you do with them is up to you. For despite my tongue-in-cheek introductory title, people aren't rats in a laboratory experiment; they are humans with values and choices.

The MBA dilemma

As I reflected on the challenges I faced as chief executive, and compared my experiences with what I had taught as a management academic, I came to the view that management should be taught differently. If the aim of management education is to produce managers rather than technicians, then the emphasis in most management education is wrong, and the way subjects are taught needs to be changed.

Most business courses are about the basic disciplines and functions of management—subjects such as accounting, finance, organisational behaviour, marketing, operations, information systems and strategic planning. All of these areas are now well-defined academic disciplines with learned peer-reviewed journals.

Although the discipline side of education is important, it takes more than academic knowledge to make a leader. There is another side to being a successful business leader that should be taught in MBAs and other business courses. It involves learning skills—like the ones I found so critical in my chief executive role—that answer questions such as:

* How can I give clear instructions so that people working for me understand what is expected of them (a prerequisite for good performance)? In particular, how do I do this when I have to manage a group that is older and more experienced than I am, but not as well qualified?

* How do I give honest, useful feedback on performance without destroying or demoralising an underperformer,

and how can I get the person to act on this or leave without causing a major legal or industrial problem?

* What is the best, most appropriate way to recognise good performance? When is a thank you or a small token the right thing to do? When should dollars be paid and how many?

* How do I build networks and conduct conversations to find out what is really going on in an area? How do I use this intelligence in negotiating or forging alliances inside and outside the organisation?

* How can I better understand myself, in particular the triggers that make me angry (and therefore potentially irrational and destructive) or comfortable (and hence not sufficiently rigorous and questioning)? How can I deal with criticism or bad news effectively?

* How do I figure out the politics of the situation? Although I dislike politics in organisations, political behaviour is a reality that needs to be identified and used.

* How do I negotiate in different situations? How can I learn to understand different positions and to find and convince people when there may be common ground?

* How do I get things done? Execution is considered at least as important as planning and requires selecting the right people, following up and troubleshooting when progress stalls.

* How do I communicate as a manager? After all, communication is the lifeblood of leadership, and it includes listening as well as articulating.

The skills implicit in these questions, and illustrated in my Fairfax experience, are if anything more important than management education. Consider the following quote from Dr David Morgan, who in 1990 moved from a senior role in the Australian Treasury to the chief executive position at Westpac Bank.

When I worked in Treasury about 80% of my job was to work out what was the right thing to do and maybe 20% of it was to convince people to follow that advice ... In the private sector those proportions were basically reversed — about 20% of your time was working out what is the right thing to do, and then about 80% of your time ... as the CEO, how do I get 27 000 people following me up the mountain?

David Morgan, *The Australian Financial Review Magazine*, August 2006

Morgan's quote is a reminder that management education has its shortcomings when it comes to the real world of business. The MBA emphasis is 80 per cent about what to do, and at best 20 per cent how to make it happen. Although I believe the case for changing this emphasis is clear and well supported by reviews of MBA programs worldwide, the question of how to rebalance the curriculum and teach these skills well has not been answered. Business schools have been unwilling to tackle the hard questions properly because so much human and intellectual capital has been invested in teaching and researching in specialised disciplines like finance, accounting and marketing. More importantly, teaching and researching critical skills that aren't discipline based—such as judgement, communication and people skills—is still in its infancy. But that may well be the subject of another book!

Media reform

Soon after the manuscript for this book had been completed, the Howard Government passed Australia's most significant media deregulation in twenty years. The new law, passed in October 2006, will relax restrictions on cross-media holdings and remove the special restrictions on foreign ownership of media, although proposals will be subject to approval by the Treasurer. The reforms are only partial and will not be enacted until an as-yet-unspecified date in 2007. But they have made it possible for media players to do deals that were not possible before. Under the new laws, each commercial radio, television and print media company will be free to link up with one other media type, provided at least five commercial players remain in capital cities and four in regional markets.

The changes unleashed an immediate frenzy of takeover speculation and sharemarket activity as media companies positioned themselves for an industry shake-up. Just hours after the government announced its reforms, James Packer's Publishing and Broadcasting Ltd sprang into action, selling half of a package comprising most of its media assets to a private equity firm. There was immediate speculation that Packer was preparing for a tilt at Fairfax, but little evidence. Packer could just as easily have been seizing the opportunity to reduce his exposure to the decaying free-to-air television market while prices were high, thus freeing up $4.5 billion to expand his interests in the growing international gaming and entertainment market.

On the same day, Kerry Stokes, owner of the Seven Network, bought a stake in West Australian Newspapers. A day later, Rupert Murdoch's News Corporation swooped on Fairfax and emerged with a 7.5 per cent holding. Then Irish media magnate Tony O'Reilly's Independent News & Media foreshadowed a private equity takeover of APN News & Media, Australia's fourth-largest media group. The next week News Ltd emerged as the buyer of a major stake in the Hannan family's suburban magazine and newspaper business. There is speculation about the intent behind all these moves but, at the time of writing, no conclusive evidence. Media companies not involved in the early manoeuvring were also caught up in the game of media hypotheticals. Fairfax, Rural Press, Channel 10 and Telstra were some of the bigger names tipped as potential predators or prey.

During my time at Fairfax I lived with tight government restrictions on cross-media holdings and foreign ownership. Despite these restrictions I also lived with constant speculation that Fairfax was vulnerable to a takeover or breakup.

The old rules were set up in 1987 by the Hawke Labor Government. Then-treasurer Paul Keating quipped at the time that you could be a prince of print or a queen of the screen, but not both. Media companies were prevented from owning more than one type of media outlet in a single market. Newspaper, radio and television companies were prohibited from owning more than 15 per cent of each other. In addition, foreign companies could not own more than 15 per cent of a television station or more than 25 per cent of a newspaper publisher.

Many people thought these restrictions were important to Fairfax because it protected the group from acquisitive people like Sir Ron Brierley of Brierley Investments, Conrad Black, Rupert Murdoch and the late Kerry Packer. A self-appointed group called the 'Friends of Fairfax' were vociferous in defending the media-ownership rules because they believed the rules ensured diversity of media ownership and the editorial independence of the *Herald* and *The Age*. I thought they were well intentioned but misguided.

On many occasions during my seven years at Fairfax I publicly advocated the removal of the media-ownership rules. I made countless submissions to parliamentary subcommittees, saw senior politicians privately and spoke on the issue at the National Press Club. My message was always the same.

First and foremost, Australia's media-ownership rules were not in Fairfax's interest; they limited the company's options and restricted its size. By limiting options to expand in the home market and restricting outside competition there was less incentive to innovate. As a result, previous boards and management of Fairfax focused almost entirely on the declining *Herald* and *Age* newspaper businesses, rather than searching for new opportunities that would grow the company and reduce its dependence on these mature assets. Size is an important factor in a company's willingness to take risks. Rupert Murdoch could afford to take more risks in both his newspaper and digital businesses than Fairfax could. To lose $100 million is little more than a rounding error to Murdoch, but for a Fairfax CEO it is a hanging offence.

The upshot of these restrictions was that media proprietors either moved offshore or expanded into areas other than media, or both. Murdoch's News Corp is now effectively a US company and Publishing and Broadcasting Ltd, under James Packer, has been moving aggressively into gaming both locally and offshore. During my seven years at Fairfax my most significant investment was offshore—the $1.1 billion purchase of the New Zealand-based INL publishing group. I believe that any government policy that restricts domestic business and forces local companies offshore is not good policy.

The second reason I supported the removal of ownership restrictions was that I wasn't unduly worried about being taken over. Fairfax would be a hard company to break up because its businesses are intertwined. Printing, pre-press, advertising sales, back-office functions, management and office space were shared. There was also a lot of cross-marketing, cross-advertising and selling. If you were to break the business up, costs would go up immediately.

I also thought Fairfax was fairly priced, which is another protection against takeover. When the company conducted its first share buyback and placement at Fairfax early in 1999 at $3.10 a share it was underpriced, but the share price moved up fairly quickly afterwards, reducing the premium available to acquirers. After the New Zealand INL purchase, Fairfax's shares moved below what I believed was fair value, but the market and media sentiment about the acquisition was quite negative, so no-one was interested in a takeover. As the value of the New Zealand purchase became apparent, the shares moved back into the $4-plus zone, which I believed made a hostile acquisition and break up of assets unlikely unless an irrational purchaser showed up. Murdoch paid $5.20 a share for his 7.5 per cent strategic stake in October 2006. Even if a takeover offer had been made on my watch, I didn't necessarily think that was a bad thing. A new owner and a new board and management need not necessarily be worse for consumers and investors than the incumbents.

Now that new media-ownership options have been created, the sharemarket value of media companies has lifted. Although there is a speculative element in the early sharemarket activity, there will likely be a more permanent increase in the underlying value of these companies. Perversely, the higher the value the stock market places on media-company shares, the less likely they are to be taken over. It won't stop takeover activity but it will stop more opportunistic bids. Some of the early market activity may have been more about staking out an option or blocking competitors than launching a takeover. In fact, my greatest concern while running Fairfax was that outside parties would acquire blocking stakes. This could stop Fairfax from making acquisitions, especially those that may involve complex finance and special resolutions requiring 75 per cent shareholder approval. In this case Fairfax would be left in a position where it would be defending declining revenue streams and seeking organic growth with only limited options.

Media reform has opened up the playing field but mergers and acquisitions must still make financial sense. I looked at some form of merger or share deal with West Australian Newspapers several times when I was at Fairfax, but I couldn't make it work. Domestic buyers or private equity firms could have made a bid for Fairfax but didn't. Under the new rules acquirers have the ability to combine any two print, television and radio assets, and yet although I can see some useful synergies, I don't see compelling synergies.

There is, however, a caveat to my positive reading of the broader options and improved market values now possible. Media reform is not a panacea for the fundamental issues that I wrestled with during my time at Fairfax and that my successor is still wrestling with. The drift of advertisers and readers away from metropolitan broadsheet newspapers such as the *Herald* and *The Age* will continue no matter who buys the company. The need for good management processes, cost controls and efficiencies will still be there, as will the need to recruit, train and hold talented employees. The best people will continue to be poached and this will become more acute as owners attempt to extract maximum value from their businesses. Fairfax will need to continuously innovate with new products such as the successful *the(sydney)magazine* to keep readers engaged in a digital age. The digital business must still be developed in an increasingly competitive environment.

I believe the media landscape has changed for the better. Over the longer term there will undoubtedly be a realignment of media interests. But from a consumer's point of view I think changes of ownership will be positive. The important shift will be that owners of the assets will be financially sound, and more able and willing to expand. Hence, media companies can and will offer better technology options for news, entertainment and communication of views and ideas. Diversity will continue and may even be enhanced, but in different forms.

Appendix A: Fairfax share prices compared with Rural Press and Seven Network share prices

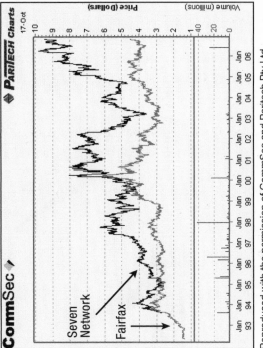

Reproduced with the permission of CommSec and Paritech Pty Ltd

Seven Network share prices compared with Fairfax share prices 1993–2006

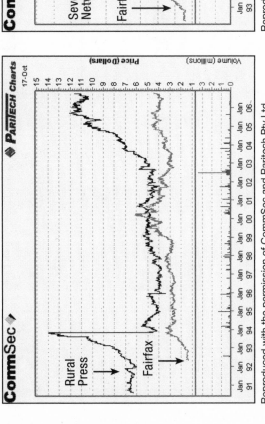

Reproduced with the permission of CommSec and Paritech Pty Ltd

Rural Press share prices compared with Fairfax share prices 1991–2006

Appendix B: International newspaper companies – annualised total shareholder returns* 1998–2005

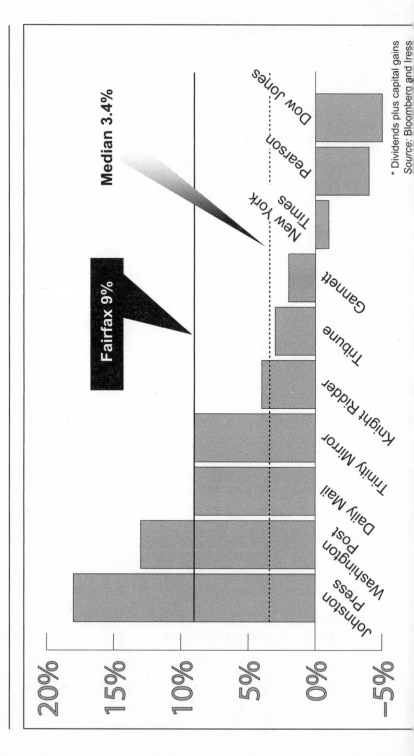

Median 3.4%

Fairfax 9%

Johnston Press
Washington Post
Daily Mail
Trinity Mirror
Knight Ridder
Tribune
Gannett
New York Times
Pearson
Dow Jones

20%
15%
10%
5%
0%
-5%

* Dividends plus capital gains
Source: Bloomberg and Iress

Appendix C: The Buffett tenets for success

Business tenets

The business must:

- be simple and understandable
- have a consistent operating history
- have favourable long-term prospects.

Management tenets

Management must:

- be rational
- remain candid with shareholders
- be able to avoid 'the institutional imperative' to resist change and follow industry practices unthinkingly.

Financial tenets

Approaches to finance should:

- focus on return on equity
- calculate 'owner earnings' (income plus depreciation less stay-in-business fixed and working capital expenditure)
- include a search for high profit margins
- ensure a dollar invested produces a dollar of value.[11]

Appendix D: The classic textbook formula for success

Strategic position

- establish a significant competitive advantage in an industry conducive to at least average profitability
- defend and extend your competitive advantage aggressively.

People

- employ the right people
- motivate your staff effectively
- set clear goals and manage and reward employees in line with performance.

Customers

- stay close to customers and know their needs intimately
- delight customers
- use customers as a key source of motivation.

Financial discipline

- allocate capital only to areas where value can be created
- recognise that capital is a scarce commodity.

Appendix E: Fairfax's organisational structure — 1998

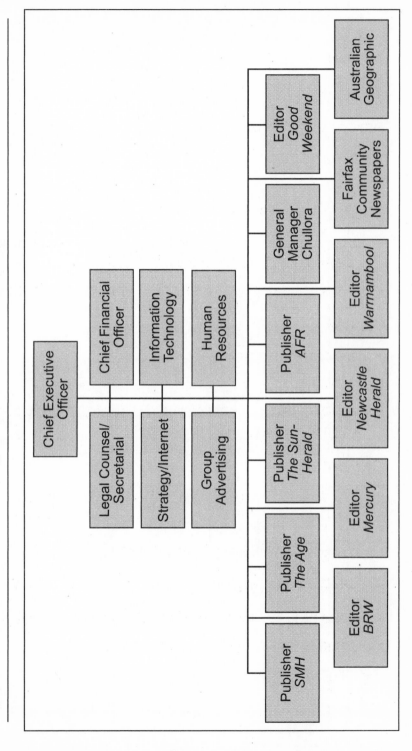

Appendix F: Fairfax's organisational structure — 1999

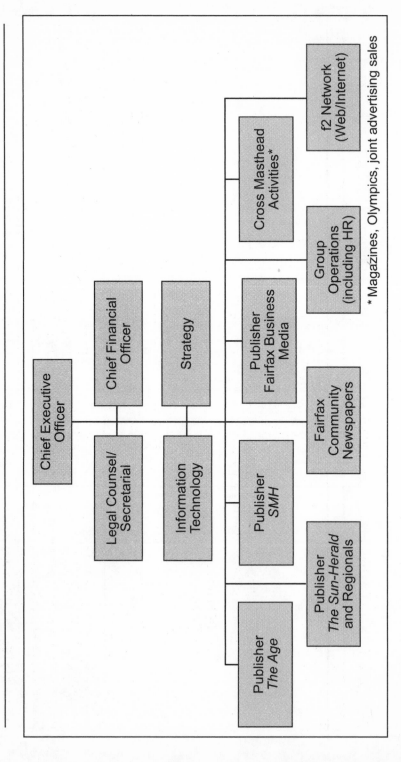

* Magazines, Olympics, joint advertising sales

Appendix G: Fairfax's organisational structure – 2003–2004

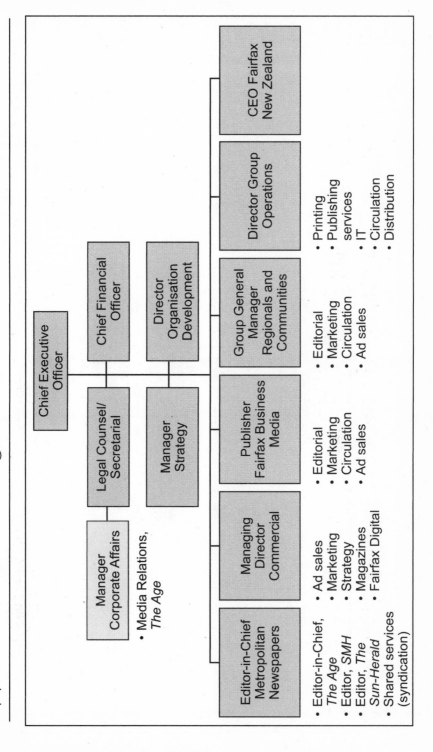

Appendix H: Fairfax's organisational structure – 2005

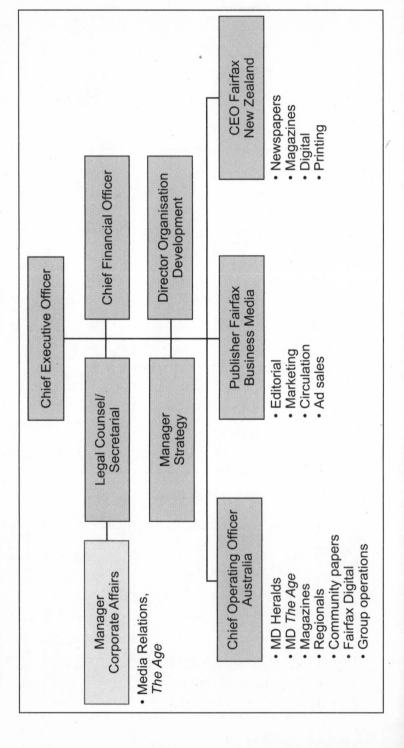

Chief Executive Officer

Manager Corporate Affairs
- Media Relations, *The Age*

Legal Counsel/ Secretarial

Chief Financial Officer

Manager Strategy

Director Organisation Development

Chief Operating Officer Australia
- MD Heralds
- MD *The Age*
- Magazines
- Regionals
- Community papers
- Fairfax Digital
- Group operations

Publisher Fairfax Business Media
- Editorial
- Marketing
- Circulation
- Ad sales

CEO Fairfax New Zealand
- Newspapers
- Magazines
- Digital
- Printing

Appendix I: Sample pages from my 2004 business diary

A 'normal' day

8.00–9.00	Phone/preparation/reading
9.00–10.00	Warren Phillips (finance)
10.30–11.00	Morgan Stanley (possible acquisition)
11.00–12 noon	Rob Antulov (strategy, review of acquisition)
12.30–2.00	Lunch — Mark Bayliss (CFO)
2.30–3.30	Treasury team (fundraising)
3.30–4.30	Meet institutional shareholder
5.30–7.30	James Hooke (review regional/community paper issues)
7.30–9.00	Phone/reading
7.30–9.00	Meet senior executives from the *Trading Post*

An investor briefing day

8.30–9.00	Briefing on investor meetings
9.00–10.00	BT Financial
10.15–11.15	Maple Brown Abbot
11.30–12.30	Lazard Asset Management
12.30–2.15	Credit Suisse lunch — address about fifteen to twenty investors
2.30–3.30	ING Investment Management
3.45–4.45	UBS Asset Management
5.00–6.00	Colonial First State

Notes

1 J Collins, *Good to Great*, HarperCollins, New York, 2001.

2 A Marcus, *Big Winners and Big Losers*, Wharton School Publishing, New Jersey, 2006.

3 GJ Stigler, *Memoirs of an Unregulated Economist*, University of Chicago Press, Chicago, 2003.

4 M Porter, *Competitive Strategy*, Simon & Schuster, New York, 1998.

5 RG Hagstrom Jr, *The Warren Buffett Way*, John Wiley & Sons, Ltd, New York, 1995.

6 J Collins, op. cit.

7 ibid.

8 JS Hammond, RL Keeney and H Raiffa, *Smart Choices*, Harvard Business School Press, Boston, 1999.

9   L Bossidy and R Charan, *The Discipline of Getting Things Done*, Crown Books, New York, 2002.

10 EG Clauser, *The Toyota Phenomenon*, Swiss Deming Institute, Zurich, 2005.

11 RG Hagstrom Jr, op. cit.

Index

acquisitions, Fairfax
—AAPT 72
—Australian Geographic 72, 107–108
—CitySearch 79, 120
—INL 23, 77–78, 99–100, 112, 134
—RSVP dating site 72, 79
—Strategic Publishing 63, 72
—Text Publishing 72
—Trade Me 72
active selling 60–61
Allen, Woody 8
Australian Consolidated Press Holdings 16
Australian Graduate School of Management 2, 6, 12, 57, 88
—confronting traditional values at 126–127

Australian Manufacturing Workers' Union 74
Australian media industry, 7, 68, 78, 90, 94, 103, 145,147
Australian Shareholders' Association 92
AWB 123

Bayliss, Mark 93, 142
Black, Conrad 16, 169
Brierley, Sir Ron 16, 169
Buffett, Warren 37
—business strategies of 38, 41, 43, 140–141, 175
Business Media 15, 53, 65, 89

Channel 7 90, 168, 173
Channel 9 148

Channel 10 90, 168
chief executive officers
—media scrutiny of 102–104, 146
—tasks 7–8, 88
—tenures 54
—time pressures on 88–92
Chullora printing plant, the 74–76, 144
classified advertising revenue, loss of 20, 24, 53, 60, 71
Coca-Cola Amatil 24–25
Collins, Jim 39, 40, 47, 107
communicating with staff 150–151
consolidation and rationalisation at Fairfax 21, 76–80
cost cutting at Fairfax 57, 58–59, 94, 113–114, 137
—Project Hercules 55–57
cross-media ownership
see also media legislation reform 3, 5, 137, 169–170

Daily Mail Company 22, 82, 137
decision making 4, 87–104, 108, 101-104, 107–108
—emotional capital and 102, 123–124
—media scrutiny and its effect on 102–104
digital challenge, 17, 20–21
Domain 64
Dunlap, Al 115,147

emotional capital see decision making
Evans, Brian 66, 67, 82, 99–100
Express 62, 122

Fairfax
—accounting at 92–93, 142
—competition 20–21, 24, 41–43, 48, 76,
—confronting traditions at 126–127
—journalistic culture 2, 17, 18, 29–30, 43, 49, 58, 69–73, 92–96
—enterprise bargaining agreements with journalists 26–27
—eroding market share 23–26, 60, 42
—first impressions 14–16
—history 13, 15
—infrastructure 30–31, 73–76
—management processes 27–28, 67–69
—market position 41–43, 48
—organisational politics 7
—organisational structure 28–29, 64–66, 82
—ownership and leadership instability 7, 13, 76
—problems 17–31, 35–36
—rising costs 26–27, 55
—sharemarket activity and 16, 18, 22, 81, 170
Fairfax board
—composition 16
—views of 17–18, 66–67, 77, 79, 128, 137

Fairfax, Warwick 15
firing or retrenching staff 148–150
Foster's Group 2, 23, 143
Friedman, Thomas 22
Friends of Fairfax 169

Gannett 22
Gill, Michael 66
Good Weekend magazine 28, 55, 56
Graham, Donald 21

Hambly, Gail 12, 66
Harley-Davidson 25–26
Hilmer's successor, the search for
    66–67
Hywood, Greg 25

Iaccoca, Lee 134
industrial action 72, 73–75
ineffective strategies 46–47
international newspaper companies,
    results of 22, 81, 174

Johnston, Craig 74
Johnston Press 22
journalism, independent 2, 18, 23, 30,
    44, 64, 152
judgement, role of 96–101
    —emotional capital and *see*
        decision making
    —market judgements 99–100
    —people judgements 96–98

Kirk, David 66–67
Knight Ridder 22

leadership, strong 157–166
    —born or made debate 163–166
    —characteristics of 159–162
        –brains 159–160, 163
        –determination 161, 163
        –energy 160, 163
        –ethics 162, 163
        –trust 161, 163
Lowy, Frank 41, 92, 96, 146, 160

management education 87–88, 164
    —gap between theory and
        practice 87, 104, 164–166
Mansfield, Bob 12
Marcus, Alfred 38–39

Matheson, Jardine 11
McKinsey & Co. 2, 6, 12, 19, 55, 56,
    88, 124, 140, 144, 145, 148
media legislation reform 5, 90,
    167–172
    see also cross-media ownership
metropolitan broadsheets, problems
    facing 24, 137
Moore-Wilton, Max 115
Morgan, David 165–166
Motorola 47
Mulholland, Stephen 12
Murdoch, Lachlan 76
Murdoch, Rupert 58, 77, 96, 103, 115,
    138, 147, 169, 170
Muscat, Bob 11, 12, 14, 156

Narayan, Sankar 142
negatives, dealing with 97, 108,
    110–113, 123, 138
    —perception and 139–145
        –questions, importance of
            140–143
        –the corporate cocoon and 141
    —persistence and 145–147
    —persuasion and 150–152
News Ltd 6, 12, 18, 23, 68, 168
    —relationship with Fairfax 62, 63,
        75–76, 78, 91

owner-shareholders 138

Packer 79–80, 90, 138
    —James 79, 80, 90, 102, 138, 168,
        169
    —Kerry 3, 11, 16, 19, 58, 77,
        79, 80, 96, 115, 138, 147, 169
performance reviews 114, 124–126
    —McKinsey & Co. and 124
Porter, Michael 41

positive bias 5, 105–129
—sources of 115–122
  –focus on dramatic events 122
  –overconfidence trap 121–122
  –seeing no evil 117–118
  –seeing what you want to *see* 120–121
  –status quo trap 118–119
  –sunk cost trap 119–120
Powers, Brian 2, 3, 12, 15, 16, 19, 89
—public commitment to shareholders 55–56
process engineering 57–58
Publishing and Broadcasting Ltd 18, 19, 23, 68, 79–80, 119, 168, 169
—relationship with Fairfax 77, 103, 146

Redstone, Sumner 159–160, 161
results, Fairfax's financial 7, 80–82
Rio Tinto 161
Rural Press Ltd 22, 77, 90, 168, 173

Scott, Mark 82
seek.com 122
Simon, Herbert 100
Stokes, Kerry 138, 168

sustained business success
—keys to 40–47
  –customer relationships 44–45
  –financial discipline 45–46
  –people 43–44
  –strong market position 41–43
—rarity of 37–40

Tabcorp 138
The Age 13, 15, 20, 60, 61, 62, 63, 65, 71, 73, 76, 77, 95, 97, 98, 113, 119, 122, 137, 169,171

theage(melbourne)magazine 63
The Australian Financial Review 13, 15, 45, 57–58, 65, 59, 110, 119
The Bulletin 146
The Central Coast Herald 62
The New York Times Company 21–22
the(sydney)magazine 63
The Sydney Morning Herald 13, 15, 24, 25, 29, 60, 61, 62, 63, 64, 65, 71, 76, 77, 80, 98, 102, 110, 112, 113, 119, 122, 127, 169, 171
The Washington Post Company 21–22, 137, 151
Thomson 137
Toyota 47, 133–134, 138, 152
—production system 135–163
  –Kaizen and 135–136
Tribune 22
Tullamarine printing plant 73–76

Waterman, Bob 145–146
Welch, Jack 41, 48, 54, 123, 155
West Australian Newspapers 22, 90, 168, 171
Westfield Group 49, 92, 160
workplace behavioural traits
—generalise, tendency to 97–98
—optimism 96–97
—passion 98